WORKING HARD IS NOT GOOD ENOUGH

Praise for the Book

'Simple and captivating...a book for people from all walks of life!'

—Tanveer Bookwala, vice president and creative producer, Balaji Motion Pictures

'Provides unique insights into transformational behaviour by addressing the often missed fundamental question, where do I start?'

—Dr Venkat K. Pedibhotla, project manager, Sygenta Corporation, NC–USA

'If you want to excel in life, read this book.'

—Santosh Thundiyil, director of photography, Hindi film industry

'A book that combines hard work with insights!'

—Naren Thimmiah, master chef, Taj Gateway Hotels, Bangalore

'A practical book that captures insights gleaned from many, helps you understand the art of upward mobility.'

—Alok Bardiya, Cisco Ventures & M&A, India and Asia-Pacific

'Terrific read, insightful and offers a refreshing perspective.'

—Alok Goel, partner, Helion Venture Partners

'Perfect recipe of insights from many who went beyond working hard.'

—Harpreet Grover, CEO and cofounder, www.cocubes.com

'This book makes you rethink all over again!'

—Sreekanth, AK, vice president, HR, Computer Sciences Corporation (CSC)

'This book will make you think and feel, simultaneously!'

—Alok Mehta, executive vice president, Global Human Resources, Intas Pharmaceuticals

TGC PRASAD

An imprint of Penguin Random House

PORTFOLIO

USA | Canada | UK | Ireland | Australia
New Zealand | India | South Africa | China | Singapore

Portfolio is part of the Penguin Random House group of companies
whose addresses can be found at global.penguinrandomhouse.com

Published by Penguin Random House India Pvt. Ltd
4th Floor, Capital Tower 1, MG Road,
Gurugram 122 002, Haryana, India

First published by Random House India in 2013
This edition published in Portfolio by Penguin Random House India 2020

10 9 8 7 6 5 4 3 2

ISBN 9788184003239

For sale in the Indian Subcontinent only

Typeset in Electra LT by R. Ajith Kumar

Printed at Manipal Technologies Limited, India

www.penguin.co.in

Rev. Prof. P.S. Satsangi Sahab

'In hard work is happiness.'

—David McCullough, two-time Pulitzer Prize winner

CONTENTS

PREFACE

FIRSTLY, THIS BOOK IS for people who find happiness and a sense of satisfaction in working hard. If you are looking at honing your insights over and above the hard work that you put in, then you probably will gain substantially from this book.

Coming to the gist of it, I have seen students, teachers, executives, professionals, and people from all walks of life working really hard. That is the fundamental bedrock on which success can be built and sustained. But then only a few people end up being perceivably successful. In my own experience as a management professional, I have seen people soar, build companies, start ventures, get better hikes, and land up with regular promotions and enriching global career opportunities, and on the flipside, I have seen people fall, stagnate, and some even wither. For a while, I pondered and tried figuring out what makes people really successful. I read many books, researched, discussed with umpteen executives and professionals, burnt the midnight oil, and wrote copious notes. In some cases, as they say, average people struck gold, some beat the path with sheer grit, a few excelled with the might of their competence, some even stumbled upon success being early risers in a new market, a few others made their fortune inventing something new, and some connected the dots and arrived at their destination. Interestingly, some sailed on the boat led by stalwarts, as a tag-along, and made their fortunes and they were smart to do that. Some perhaps were fortunate enough to inherit both wealth and talent and put it to the cartwheel. In any case, I soon realized that there was no cookie cutter approach to being successful. But then, there are some behaviours, competencies, some management methods, perhaps a combination of some and maybe all, in a given context, if applied well, can potentially lead to success. Here, in this book, I reproduce a reasonable concoction for your benefit, hopefully, which will make you think.

As you read the book, don't look at one perspective, or one answer. What I have tried to do is present various perspectives, at times contradicting ones, so that one can see the paradox. As Charles Handy, a leading Irish author and philosopher, who specializes in organization behaviour, said, 'Paradoxes are to be lived with, not solved.' Importantly, in this world, there is nothing as the ultimate truth and as you read, I urge you to gather insights.

While I was penning down this book, as I have done with my earlier book, *Unusual People Do Things Differently*, I kept the stories and real life examples on the foreground and kept pure theory at bay, because people understand metaphors and stories easily. Besides, I relish storytelling. Importantly, I have attempted to retain real names and examples, and at times, for the right reasons, have changed names of people, companies, etc.

Introduction

THIS BOOK TRIES TO explore that edge, over and above the hard work, which people anyway put in, and tries to offer insights to enable you to think.

Before you read any further, let me get a caveat out of the way–it is futile to not work hard and try implementing other methods to succeed. That is like, not exercising at all and wondering why you aren't fit enough. Hard work is like working on how to lose the acquired calories by walking ten miles; while smart work is not piling them on, in the first place. This book addresses what you do besides walking those ten miles. It is about being smart enough to plan the marathon. Hopefully this book should gradually turn you into a smarter thinker, an edge that perhaps you always wanted to have. But please don't expect miracles. It takes nine months to deliver a baby; nine mothers cannot deliver a baby in one month! You may perhaps already know many of the aspects mentioned here, in which case, it becomes a point of re-emphasis, a succinct summary, for you to remember.

Competition at workplace; or to get a glimpse, or perhaps even to pass through portals of institutions of higher learning, is so daunting that almost everybody you meet across the street or in the hallway is burning the midnight oil. Best of skills need to be honed under the soft gaze of the table-lamp and with every turn of the page. Ten thousand hours is what it takes to be an expert, says Malcolm Gladwell[1], a British–Canadian journalist and bestselling author. At forty hours a week, it is almost four-and-a-half years of sustained work on a specific area to gain expertise. Basically, it is a combination of sustained hard work, getting smarter at what you do, and most importantly figuring out what to attempt and what to keep aside.

Scores of executives thronging office cubicles, countless aspiring students who flock university admission offices seeking higher education—all of them put endless hours and only a few manage to be successful. Only few get to the Ivy League universities, a few create world-class products and companies, only some have the ability to develop newer technologies, and only a handful stumble upon a diamond in their backyard. How is it that only a few seem to always land early bird offers? Possibly some of these people who made the cut, exhibit certain key behaviours, possess certain vital skills, or probably know how to steer, garner, build, and retain talent, or perhaps are able to strategize and can crystal gaze into the future. Probably some of these people have the ability to see opportunities far ahead of the curve. Or do they recognize patterns better than the others. Some possibly are experts at how to turbo-charge their performance when it is needed the most. Is it persistence, energy, strategy, vision, execution, creativity, innovation, smart thinking, diversity, inclusiveness, advocacy, or some part of or combination of all these?

There are so many variables out there, and there are also exceptions in the form of geniuses. People expressed that he wasn't as laudable with people, but Steve Jobs, ex-CEO of Apple Inc. coined a phrase called 'bozo explosion', where managers become polite and mediocre stick around. He said, 'I don't think I run roughshod with people, but if something sucks, I am honest in giving it to them.' But then exceptions are allowed for geniuses. You won't grudge Steve Jobs for recreating Apple, isn't it! According to a *Harvard Business Review* article of January–February 2013, during his tenure with Apple, between 1997–2011, Steve Jobs produced the highest market capitalization of nearly $360 billion and the country's adjusted shareholder returns grew by 6682 percent with an average compound annual growth rate of 35 percent. That is an exceptional record by any standard and a business icon to reckon with. And guess what, he was a true hard worker.

Most people work hard, but less than 2 percent of entrepreneurs are people you hear about, less than one percent become great leaders, about less than 1 percent make it as CEOs, very few create the highest shareholder value, only 15 percent get the best performance ratings and best pay hikes, less than 20 percent of the sales people make the best commissions, and only 15 percent get bumped up to senior levels every two to three years. How do they do it? What makes them different? How do they learn? What insights do these people have? How do they work? How do they think? This book tries to help you get a few insights and makes you think. If you apply them, perhaps you may start riding a new tide.

This book is not specific to any one industry or a cross-section of people; it is a general management book and applies to any student, executive, or professional—in short, anybody who wants to gain insights into our rapidly changing world.

The book has fifteen chapters and each covers a specific topic. The chapters were chosen based on extensive discussions with many senior people in the industry across various functions. Though there are many other topics of significance, I included only those that I believe can make a substantial impact to your thinking.

Failures to Success

'Anyone who has never made a mistake has never tried anything new.'

—**Albert Einstein**

ACCEPTING FAILURES IS EASIER said than done, because the human ego doesn't permit accepting failures. Besides it is a lonely path to walk, and many people shirk to support others during times of failure. People network only if you are successful, and when you fall, people find reasons to be busy to keep away from you. That is an unsaid law in this world. Given the scenario associated with failures, people end up building strong walls internally and avoid taking risks and experimentation takes a back seat. This leads to people following routines, since it provides them with a sense of security. Besides change is inevitable and it is quite daunting to crossover to the other side of the bridge. But there are people who have seen early failures, and have eventually succeeded and created substantial value.

Once a young man interviewed with Toyota Motor Corporation for a job as an engineer. He was turned down, leaving him jobless for quite some time. He then worked for a car mechanic for six long years doing menial tasks. With a little encouragement from friends and neighbours, he started making scooters from his home and experienced a series of failures. Eventually the business succeeded, scooters became popular and when cars were introduced, this business became a powerful competitor for Toyota. The young man was none other than Soichiro Honda, founder of Honda Motor Company. Soichiro Honda[1] says, 'Success is 99 percent failure.' He also said, 'There is a Japanese proverb that literally goes like this "Raise the sail with your stronger hand", meaning you must go after the opportunities that arise in life that you are best equipped to do.'

I have not come across any successful entrepreneur, businessman, sports-personality, or career professional, who has not seen failures. Almost every successful person who fell, took failure in his stride and emerged successful. Some of these people were determined to succeed. To that extent, before taking the decision to fund, venture capitalists and private equity players give a higher score to entrepreneurs who have failed earlier and are still striving to get on with the next failure. The zeal shows and that is a sense of relief for an investor.

Reviewing the book *The Survivor* about Bill Clinton, former president of the US, on May 31, 2005, *The New York Times* published an article titled, 'Two Terms of Chaos, Comebacks and Crises'. It quotes Bill Clinton saying, 'Do you know who I am?', a question Bill Clinton asked his adversary Newt Gingrich during the government shutdown of 1995–96. He answered the question himself, 'I'm the big rubber clown doll you had as a kid, and every time you hit it, it bounces back.' 'The harder you hit me,' he added, 'the faster I come back up.' Even during the worst time of his life, and during a personal crisis, when his friends and the whole world was trying to write him off, he knew he would come out of the low he was going through. He was determined to survive; he was resolute to get the American administration going during the rest of his term. Perhaps that left a big scar on him, his family, and the American presidency. But after leaving office in 2001, as a private citizen, he knew exactly what he wanted to do. Today, the Clinton Foundation, as a part of its global initiative, has improved the lives of 400 million people with about 2,100 commitments valued at $69.2 billion in more than 180 countries. As on December 31, 2011, the total revenues generated by the foundation is upwards of $250 million, 12 million people globally have been provided with job opportunities, it has enabled

3.5 million children to eat and live healthier lives, and nearly 4 million AIDS affected people are benefiting from drugs purchased at reduced prices. How inspirational is that, from rising over the challenges that life throws at you to marching forward to serve humanity?

Nelson Mandela[2] was arrested in 1962 and was imprisoned for 27 years. During his prison tenure, he undertook study and completed his Bachelor of Laws from University of London under its distance education programme. Even under extreme duress as a D-class prisoner, who was allowed one letter and one visitor every six months, he never lost heart and was revered as the most powerful black leader in South Africa. On his release, he became the president of ANC and conducted negotiations with president F.W. de Klerk and both were jointly awarded the Nobel Peace Prize in 1993. In 1994, ANC won with 62 percent majority and Nelson Mandela became the first black president and the oldest one at the age of 75. A third of his life was spent in prison, yet he didn't see himself as a failure or let the incarceration affect him.

It needs a focused and clear mind to pursue an objective and see beyond successes and failures. I believe success and failure is just a perception, what matters more to such people is the attainment of an ultimate goal, a vision that expands beyond the horizons of judgmental human perceptions.

Most people don't know this, but after dropping out from Harvard, Bill Gates, along with cofounder Paul Allen started 'Traf-O-Data', which failed. This was followed by more ideas, eventually ending with the founding of Microsoft, a company which needs no introduction. Quarter ending June 30, 2012, Microsoft generated revenues of $73.72 billion and an operating income of $21.76 billion. The operating income of Microsoft is more than the GDP of countries like Estonia, Bolivia, Uganda, Ghana, Brunei, Honduras, Paraguay, Afghanistan, Senegal, Nepal, Zambia, Jamaica, Iceland, and Albania etc. Market capitalization as on December 31, 2012, is $270.64 billion dollars.

The point is—it doesn't matter if you fail. That is a part of life. Rise above the failures, learn from them, and keep experimenting and inventing with ideas—your chances of success will increase manifold.

Walt Disney[1], the creator of Disney characters like Mickey Mouse saw more failures than the successes he anticipated. As on April 5, 2013, Disney's market capitalization was about $102.25 billion. Ending in December 2012, Disney's revenues stood at $42.28 billion with an operating income of $8.76 billion. Surprisingly, a newspaper editor had fired Walt Disney because he lacked imagination and had no good ideas. After that Disney started a number of businesses that didn't last too long and ended in failure and bankruptcy. However, he continued his efforts and made the first full-length animation movie, *Snow White and the Seven Dwarfs*, which no distributor was willing to take up, and they had to be cajoled with huge discounts. When the movie opened, it made history and Walt Disney established a prominent place for himself in history.

Apparently, the rice cooker was the first product introduced into the market by Akio Morita, the co-founder of Sony Corporation. It sold a total of hundred units and often the contents of the cooker were burned. The failure didn't dent the confidence of Akio and his partners. They surged forward with newer products to create Sony Corporation, a multi-billion dollar company.

Let us take examples of some world famous geniuses and thinkers. Charles Darwin[1] was viewed as dim-witted, lazy, and a dreamer. He almost failed college. Charles Darwin wrote, 'I was considered by all my masters and my father, a very ordinary boy, rather below the common standard of intellect.' As years passed, his keen sense of observation and patient research led him to the seminal work on the survival of the species.

You will be surprised to note that Thomas Edison[1] was fired from two jobs for not being productive enough. Edison tried a thousand times at inventing the light bulb and failed every time. But that did not deter him and eventually he designed the light bulb that worked. Interestingly, his teachers said, 'Edison is too stupid to learn anything.'

Albert Einstein[1] did not speak until he was four, and could not read until he was seven. His parents and teachers thought he was challenged. He was expelled from school and was refused admission to the famous Zurich Polytechnic Institute. Later in his life, he earned his living as a clerk and toiled many a nights to become the father of modern physics and eventually won a Nobel Prize.

The Wright brothers[1] battled family illness, depression, and extended stays at home. They started a bicycle shop and eventually from 1900s onwards experimented with flights. For several years they toiled hard, and tried different kinds of prototypes, flying machines, and gliders. But all their attempts went in vain and they failed miserably umpteen times before their first flight took off on December 17, 1903, from Kitty Hawk, North Carolina. When they initially wrote to the US Government, the military dismissed their claims of the possibility of a flying machine. They were the first to institute a three-axis control that is still used today for fixed wing aircrafts. Failure didn't dent their enthusiasm to create the first flight; instead it instigated them further to succeed. That is the kind of motivation you need if you want to succeed. Keep trying till you see a major difference and that needs persistence.

Winston Churchill[1] said, 'Success is the ability to go from one failure to another with no loss of enthusiasm.' Interestingly, Winston Churchill struggled in school and failed his sixth grade. He was elected twice as the prime minister of United Kingdom, but struggled during the cold period of politics between 1929 and 1933, when his party lost the election and he was never invited to occupy any post in the government. He also lost the general elections in 1945, when he failed to convince the British populace of his strategies and plans. With advancing age and after having suffered several strokes after 1946, he continued to campaign and won the general elections in 1951 to become the prime minister of Britain. In 1955, he received the Nobel Prize for Literature for the book *The Second World War*. In the same year he took retirement from politics because of health reasons.

The meaning of life is to see the ups and downs to gain wisdom and not to be perturbed by the vagaries of it. Success is a long journey and that one moment when it presents itself as a bowl of opportunity, realization dawns, but then that is fleeting. Plodding is the essence of a nicer crop, season after season and year after year. Failures are lessons that make you stronger to sustain success. For success one has to prepare hard. Here is an interesting quote by coach John Wooden, 'Failing to prepare is preparing to fail.'

All India Radio rejected Amitabh Bachchan, the icon

of Indian cinema, because he didn't have a good voice, and today his baritone is recognized by almost a billion people in the subcontinent. Most motion picture directors refused to cast him because of his height (6 feet 2 inches) and lanky looks. He didn't give up his pursuit to be an actor. Probably the rejections egged him further to be one of India's finest actors. To that extent, he was such a prominent figure in Indian cinema in 1970s and 1980s that French director Francois Truffaut called him a 'one man industry'. Very few see success of that nature and at times it could be very heady. Subsequently, in 1996, he started ABCL—a company to produce movies, television programmes, distribute and manage media, etc. In the same year with the debacle of Miss India pageant held at Bangalore, for which ABCL was the main sponsor, he got into serious financial difficulties, where Mumbai High Court even restrained him from selling some of his residential assets, pending clearance of dues to banks. However, he revived his career by anchoring the popular TV quiz show, 'Kaun Banega Corepati' (Who Wants to be a Millionaire) and subsequently Yash Chopra, a famous movie producer, offered him a role as the stern patriarch of an esteemed residential school, in the movie, *Mohabbatein*, and that swung his trajectory once again. He took failures in his stride, moved on, and focused on what he has always been good at—entertaining people!

Oprah Gail Winfrey[3] was born on January 29, 1954,

and as explained by her, her birth resulted from a single sexual encounter between her teenage parents—her mother Vernita Lee, who worked as a maid, and her father Vernon Winfrey, a coal miner turned into a barber. Oprah revealed to her viewers in the 1986 talk show that, when she was nine years old, her cousin, her uncle, and a family friend, molested her. At 13, after suffering years of abuse, she ran away from home and at 14, she conceived and delivered a baby boy who died at infancy. She faced numerous career setbacks and was even fired from her job as a television reporter because she was 'unfit for Television'. Times changed, persistence paid, and in 2008, she was probably responsible for bringing in a million votes to the Obama campaign. She has been ranked the richest African–American of the 20th century and her net worth earning in 2012 is estimated at close to $2.7 billion. Apparently her grandmother Hettie Mae influenced her, and she says, 'Gave me a positive sense of myself.'

After having read biographies of so many successful people who have risen from the ashes of failures, I strongly believe that having a strong, positive sense about oneself drives people to lift themselves from the throes of failure and to eventually become successful.

At 17, Sydney Poitier[4], amongst American cinema's greatest legends, went to New York, did menial jobs, and slept in a bus terminal toilet. He then had a brief stint in the army as a worker and performed menial jobs in Harlem and New York. After his first audition, he was told by the casting director, 'Why don't you stop wasting people's time and go out and become a dishwasher or something?' Poitier decided to improve his accent and performance and dedicated the next six months to overcoming his failures. In his second attempt, he got accepted and was given a small part in a Broadway production, *Lysistrata* for which he got excellent reviews. In 1963, he became the first black man to win an Academy Award, for his role as Homer Smith in the movie, *Lilies of the Field*.

I am fascinated by the simplicity of his thoughts when he said, 'A good deed here, a good deed there, a good thought here, a good comment there, all added up to my career in one way or another.' It occurs to me that people who have emerged successful from difficult circumstances had 'goodness in their heart'. I guess this is another important facet to career—a good heart is always welcome by people. Often business of life is not completed in a series of mechanical transactions; it perhaps starts with a good heart and ends with a greater heart to serve.

J.K. Rowling[1], author of the *Harry Potter* series, is one of the most popular writers of the 21st century. But before she published the series, she was almost penniless, depressed, divorced, and was doing her best to raise a child on her own while attending school and writing a novel. In a span of five years, however, Rowling went from being dependent on state welfare to being one of the richest women in the world. When she was 26, she moved to Portugal. She worked on her novels during the mornings, and taught as an English teacher in the afternoons. The story about a 'wizard boy' was conceptualized around this time. After the birth of her daughter, Jessica in 1993, her marriage ended in divorce and she moved to Edinburgh, Scotland, where she decided to finish her novel and get it published. She often wrote in restaurants, where she and her daughter could stay warm while she wrote. She requested a grant from the Scottish Arts Council to complete her book. On completion, she received several rejections and had to sell the novel, *Harry Potter* and the *Philosopher's Stone*, to Bloomsbury, UK, for about $4,000. By 1997, the book took off and subsequently, the sequels were released. By the summer of 2000, she earned around $400 million and her books were printed in 35 different languages and over 30 million copies were sold.

Apparently, when the famous English boy band, 'The Beatles', was starting out, a recording company told them, 'We don't like their sound, and guitar music is on the way out', but they persisted against such rejections. They initially called themselves 'Blackjacks', and then changed their name to 'The Quarrymen', only realizing later that another local band was using the same name. During the initial auditions, they had a problem identifying the right drummer and eventually settled with Starr. Starting in 1960, for a period of three years, they played in Liverpool and Hamburg and gained some reputation, especially with the hit 'Love me Do', which they performed in 1962. But by 1964, the Beatlemania took over the entire Europe and even in the US and between 1965–70, they came up with chartbuster albums like 'Rubber Souls', 'The Beatles', 'Revolver', 'Abbey Road' and others. 'The Beatles' received seven Grammys, an Academy Award for best original score, 15 Ivor Novello Awards, and in 2008, they were featured in Billboard's Top 100 hot-list. That is the power of persistence, rising from the depths of despair of not having accomplished much to reaching the pinnacle of fame and recognition. At times, it is important to stand up against odds to make things happen. Importantly, one should pick the right odds.

Michael Jordan[1], one of the best basketball players of all times was actually thrown out of his high school basketball team. That didn't put him off though. He famously said, 'I have missed more than 9,000 shots in my career. I have lost almost 300 games. On 26 occasions, I have been entrusted to take the game winning shot, and I missed. I have failed over and over and over again in my life. And that is why I succeed.'

Jack Thomas Andraka[5], born in 1997, at the age of 16, created a diagnostic test to determine early stage pancreatic, ovarian, or lung cancer. It is a dipstick type test, and uses paper sensor like a diabetic test-strip. This test is 168 times faster, 26,000 times less expensive, 400 times more sensitive than any existing diagnostic test, and takes only 5 minutes to complete. He had no billion-dollar grants and while conducting this research, he wrote to 200 professors at various institutes and received nearly 200 rejection emails. The only positive reply he got was from Dr Anirban Maitra, Professor of Pathology, Oncology, Chemical and Bio-molecular Engineering at John Hopkins School of Medicine. For his invention, Jack won the first prize at the Intel Science Fair and was awarded the Gordon E. Moore Award for his work. Later he spoke at TED and met president Obama at the White House.

I believe that those who failed at least tried. If you are afraid of trying, you have a bigger problem to solve.

Play to Strengths

'The best way to predict your future is to create it.'

—**Peter Ferdinand Drucker**

DAN WITTERS, JIM ASPLUND, and Jim Harter of Gallup, in their September 2012 study, write that half the people in the US don't use their strengths throughout the day. Between August 23–27, 2012, Gallup polled 5,049 American adults with the question, 'About how many hours out of the day yesterday were you able to use your strengths to do what you do best?' The results indicated that a majority of Americans above 18 years of age are not able to use their strengths to do what they do best throughout the day. 57 percent responded, saying that they use their strengths for less than or equal to six hours every day. Only 25 percent reported that they use their strengths for ten hours a day. 6 percent of women used their strengths for ten hours a day compared to 23 percent of men. Women used their strengths at an average of 7.1 hours each day compared to 6.6 hours for men. Further, it was noted by the study that those who reported using their strengths optimally were better engaged, exhibited higher performance, and were less likely to quit. Also those business units where employees received feedback on their strengths were performing better compared to the others. Importantly, team members were far better engaged, profitable, and productive, when their managers received feedback on their strengths.

The review mechanism in the Indian school system has a report card, where grades are accorded for understanding and performance in all the subjects. As soon as any parent sees the grade card, his attention is automatically drawn towards the lowest grades because this is exactly what the parent's father did when the parent was a kid and so did the grandfather. For generations, it has been etched into our psyche to focus on the lowest grades and try our best to improve them. Without any exception, most parents do that. I have not come across one parent who doesn't focus on low grades. A familiar question in most households—'So, why are your mathematics grades consistently low?' The kid often has no answer. But then at the top of the chart, the kid has been consistently scoring well on social sciences. The parent looks at it, smiles and thinks, 'Social science is just fine, we need to focus on mathematics.' And for months after that, the attention shifts to mathematics. In the short run, the math scores go up a bit, but the social science scores stagnate or may even drop a bit. Importantly, most parents want their kids to get the best overall grades and that is understandable because the competition is stiff. But then the question is, 'Are we honing the strengths adequately?' So over a period of time, the kid is conditioned to getting good averages and not necessarily superlatives in the few subjects he or she is good at. Even in companies, during the year-end performance review, managers focus on the areas where people have not done well and try to improve them. If managers focused on where people are doing well and upped the benchmarks, then they would be playing to the strengths. Even training programmes focus on where people lack competence. Not many companies focus on programmes where people have a natural affinity. And the 'Gallup poll' has clearly proved that: 'a person will be most productive if we leverage on what the person is already good at—leverage the strength, rather than improve the weaknesses'.

Just the other day, I was watching a bunch of ten-year-olds. They were planning a half-day outing to a nearby park. Most accepted one of the boys as their leader since he was good at assigning tasks to people. It was coming quite naturally to him and the other boys were responding to his guidance. One other boy was drawing up lists of what to take for the outing. Another fetched maps and was drawing the route plan. Interestingly, they all came up with a perfect plan within twenty minutes. Now who taught them what roles to play? How did they decide? There were no rules nor any already decided factors. These are inherent traits that people develop early on.

It is a pity that legends have to move on. Peter Ferdinand Drucker,[1,2,3,5,6] an Austrian born American management consultant, is often referred to as the father of management. He was the Clarke Professor of Social Science and Management at Claremont University, California. He passed away on November 11, 2005. If you have read the HBR classic from March–April 1999, about 'Managing Oneself' by Peter Drucker and completely figured it out, then you can skip this chapter.

Quoting Drucker, 'Success in the knowledge economy comes to those who know themselves—their strengths, their values, and how they best perform ... History's greatest achievers—Napoleon, Da Vinci, Mozart—have always managed themselves. That, in large measure, is what makes them great achievers. But they are rare exceptions, as unusual both in their talent and their accomplishments as to be considered outside the boundaries of ordinary human existence. Now, most of us, even those of us with modest endowments, will have to learn to manage ourselves. We will have to learn to develop ourselves. We will have to place our self where we can make the greatest contribution. And we will have to stay mentally alert and engaged during a fifty year working life, which means knowing how and when to change the work we do.'

Most of us do not know what we should be doing, what will make us happy, and what our strengths are. Often we don't even think about it because we have caught the sails of a ship, which is taking us to different shores and we are enjoying the breeze and regaling ourselves with what each shore has to offer. Very few actually say, 'You know what, I don't want to get on this ship at all. I want to make mine, or I will define the shore I like to see.' Many don't take decisions or make choices.

Feedback analysis substantially helps if you are sincere about personal development. The concept dates back to German theologians of the 14th century—John Calvin, father of Calvinism, and Ignatius Loyola, founder of the Jesuit order, both arrived at this process independent of the other. Both these theologians built large institutional empires with Calvinism in northern Europe and the Jesuits in southern Europe. Drucker says, 'The routine feedback from expectations to results, reaffirming their commitment and allowing them to focus on achievement and satisfaction, is the advantage of this model.' It is a simple method, whenever you take a key decision or action, write down the expected end result, and measure it against reality in approximately a year. Collate these over a period of time and you will get to know, to a reasonable extent, what your strengths are. Combine this with passion and you will never feel that you are working hard. You will enter a zone of intense satisfaction leading to happiness.

I dreamt of meeting three people in my life and managed to meet the first two—Mother Teresa: to feel her kindness, Bill Clinton: to soak in his magnetism, and Peter F. Drucker: for grabbing a bit of this thought. Meeting giants and if possible working with them is important because they add meaning to your life. At times, these people have the ability to motivate you, which helps you succeed in the long-run. For example, after meeting Bill Clinton, I was pretty impressed with his oratory skills and in order to improvise mine, I sat late nights and watched all his videos and picked some nuances, and it proved to be beneficial. Strengths can be built upon; it needs a little dreaming, and a lot of hard work and patience to go after what you have set out to do.

Anthony K. Tjan, the managing partner and founder of the venture capital firm Cue Ball and the author of the bestselling book, *Hearts, Smarts, Guts and Luck* writes in a *Harvard Business Review* July 2012 article, 'How Leaders Become Self-aware', that in an analysis of four key traits that drive business and entrepreneurial success—heart, smarts, guts, and luck, when sampled across 500 global entrepreneurs and business builders, found that, about 50 percent were heart dominant, 25 percent luck, 15 percent guts, and 10 percent smarts. Success and failures were across all types thereby not specifically yielding the core trait that could lead to success.

Countless articles have been written on strengths that lead to success, but most don't converge to a singular set. It perhaps is a combination and that is what you have to figure out for yourself. But undoubtedly, research has conclusively proven and Drucker reiterates that, 'It takes far more energy to improve from incompetence to mediocrity than to improve from first-rate performance to excellence.' Moving on the scale from first-rate to excellence requires sharpening and moving from incompetence to mediocrity. It needs transformation and people find sharpening much easier than transforming themselves, because the former falls in their zone of affinity. Affinity, however, is nothing but a natural rhythm that most people develop inherently during the early years of their life. Drucker almost issues a directive, 'Do not try to change yourself—you are unlikely to succeed. Work to improve the way you perform.'

Magnus Carlsen, a 23-year-old Norwegian chess grandmaster and prodigy, is ranked as the No. 1 chess player in the world. In 2009, Garry Kasparov had an opportunity to train Carlsen and he says, 'His intuitive style conserves the mystic of chess at a time when every CPU-enhanced fan thinks the game is easy.' *Time* magazine named him one of the 100 most influential people and calls him the Justin Bieber of chess. His world chess federation rating, based on how a player fares against other rated players, is 2,872—the highest in chess history, more than Garry Kasparov's, which was 2,851.

Carlsen started to display his aptitude for solving intellectual challenges at a very young age. His father recounts that, at 2 years, he could solve a fifty piece jigsaw puzzle, and when he was 4-years-old, he enjoyed assembling Lego sets, which were for age group of 10–14. He learnt how to play chess, when he was 5-years-old, from his father. Carlsen played alone for hours at a time searching for combinations and replaying games over and over again.

Some people are gifted and display their intellect very early in their lives. It is important to hone your capabilities in the right direction and then people can play to their strengths. In the case of Carlsen, he has an analytical mind that could solve complex puzzles, combined with a sense of intuition and immense patience—a perfect recipe for playing chess and rightly his parents got him engaged in that game, where he became a grandmaster when he was 13-years-old.

One of the best books that I recently read is Susan Cain's bestseller, *Quiet*. Here is an interesting story from her book: It was a cool day on December 1, 1955, in Montgomery, Alabama, and on that day, Rosa Parks[4] was tired, her shoulders drooped and her legs were swollen from working long hours in the Montgomery Fair department store, ironing clothes. She went and sat in the black section of the bus. As more white passengers climbed into the bus, she was asked to abandon her seat for a white man. She quietly refused and was firm about it. When she refused, the bus driver, James Blake warned Rosa, 'If you don't stand up, I'm going to have to call the police and have you arrested.' Rosa calmly replied, 'You may do that.'

Her actions were not premeditated, but she knew that her quiet disagreement would have a stupendous effect upon the black community, especially over issues relating to racial segregation in transportation. Meanwhile a police officer arrives and he asks her, why she wouldn't vacate. She said, 'Why do you all push us around?', and the police officer says, 'I don't know. But the law is the law and you are under arrest.' And the events that unfolded have created American history. When she died in 2005, the obituaries read, 'courage of a lion', 'timid', 'shy', and Rosa Park's autobiography is titled, *Quiet Strength*.

In a world where matinee idols, charismatic leaders, fantastic orators, and magnetic personalities are aped, idolized, and celebrated, there is also enough and more space for the quiet and resilient people. There is space for writers who you will never meet, faceless designers who designed your shoes, unseen artists who painted your church dome, programmers, sitting in far off corners of the world, who coded for you to book airline tickets, engineers who built the bridge on which you drive—all of whom you will never come across. Power of voice, charisma, or oration matters in professions that need it the most and these are traits that people need not necessarily possess naturally in order to succeed. However, if you are a stage performer and extremely shy, well then, you are in the wrong profession. If you are a designer and your job is to clean up lathe machines every day, will you not end up frustrated? Cain says, 'Not every CEO or a leader is an extrovert or gregarious. That is not even expected or required. Some of the world's best performing CEOs are introverts viz., Bill Gates (Microsoft), Charles Schwab (Schwab), Brenda Barnes (Sara Lee), James Copeland (Deloitte).'

Owing to the successes of people who are excellent speakers, high octane performers and charismatic personalities often people misconstrue strengths as being outspoken, gregarious, boisterous, talkative, pushy, and such others. GE went ahead and defined 'being high-energy driven' as a corporate value and had it etched on their corporate walls. As a display of this corporate value, one of the senior executives at GE misconstrued it and was walking so fast in the corridors that I was afraid he might knock somebody down on the aisle. Unless the intent is clearly understood, it sends a wrong signal to people. Does everybody have to display that kind of high-energy? What energy would a lab technician working on urine samples, throughout the day, display? What energy would a scientist working on DNA sampling display? Both of them display quiet, persistent energy—a unique strength to possess. One mistake from them and the wrong drug could get administered.

Sometimes strong symbols of strength, especially high-testosterone charisma influence people significantly, and in the last few decades, corporate America reeled under its impact. Susan Cain writes that the 'culture of personality' overtook the 'culture of character'. 'Speak up or lose it' kind of culture started to pervade and people started imbibing personality traits, which they put on display for others to recognize, thereby progressing on the curve of happiness from adulation, a self-fulfillment of personal growth arising from external locus of control. Unfortunately, this leads to dissatisfaction.

Hitler, Stalin, and Mao are some of the most charismatic leaders of the last century, and look what they did to the world. Charismatic leadership undoubtedly is overstated. Harry Truman succeeded to American presidency on April 12, 1945, and was of a quiet demeanor, with hardly any charisma. But people who worked for him, vouched that he was the most trustworthy person one could ever meet. Working closely with the government, he was instrumental in the founding of United Nations and enacted the Marshall Plan granting $13 billion to rebuild Europe, after the Second World War. He didn't possess any charisma, but had the real inner strength which made him a decisive leader.

Real strength is the inner strength that creates a significant impact on the ease with which people perform in a certain work area. Sachin Tendulkar, one of the greatest cricketing legends with more than hundred cricket centuries to his credit, often gets compared to Brian Lara of West Indies and Don Bradman of Australia. He plays with absolute ease and doesn't over-conceptualize his play. He once remarked that he sees the approaching cricket ball, as big as a football. That makes things easy for him. His play could be a gift of nature; and perhaps he has honed his inner strengths of focus and instant reflexes over a period of time and applied it to his passion, which is cricket. Interestingly, he is quiet and shy in person.

Being an expert in one specific area and possessing an integrated knowledge around its periphery helps working in expert and diversified teams—that come out with innovative solutions. But often the intellectual depth in one area precludes one from appreciating the expertise of the other. An HR professional wouldn't appreciate the systematic measurement driven methods and tool-based approaches to solving problems and an engineer might not appreciate the intrinsic motivations of people who come together to solve a problem. Interestingly, retaining expertise in one area and cultivating a temperament of curiosity towards other domains seems to be a perfect recipe for the development of a holistic approach that could potentially pave way for leadership roles. Leaders, in the future will have to contend dealing with ambiguity, customer orientation, and innovation. But then, it is impossible for leaders to be experts at everything, so the secret of effectiveness is to leverage, rely, and assess strengths of experts and influence them towards a vision. That in itself is a significant strength to reckon with.

Wall Street was unhappy with Jeff Bezos when he focused on long-term value creation for consumers above shareholders, but after 16 years at the helm of affairs, Jeff Bezos delivered industry-adjusted shareholder results of 12,266 percent (HBR, Jan-Feb 2013). Amazon wrote, 'We are here for the long-term.' On Cyber Monday, November 26, 2012, which set an all-time record for retail sales, a space that Amazon invented, HBR's editor-in-chief Adi Ignatius, posed a question to Bezos—'How do you institutionalize the ability to come up with these good, misunderstood ideas?' His response was, 'First, there are stories we tell ourselves internally about persistence and patience, long-term thinking, staying focused on the consumer. Second, we select people who, when they wake up in the morning, are thinking about how to invent on behalf of the customer. If you like a more competitively focused culture, you might find us dull. We find our culture intensely fun. We have an explorer mentality, not a conqueror mentality.' Getting people on board with the right mindset and defining a culture for the company is a strength Bezos breathed for the last sixteen years, a unique strength to fine-tune and keep, in an industry where analysts and people are looking at results every ninety days.

Lastly, it is best to closely work and associate with successful people, because their strengths, thoughts, and best practices tend to rub off on you. In mentoring and coaching lies transference of knowledge and wisdom. If you play with grandmasters, you will end up learning a few tricks of the trade. Choose wisely whom you want to work, play, and spend time with. It determines the amount of information and learning that you can garner. Often information, over a period of time, turns into an insight, and insights over a period of time culminate into knowledge. Knowledge, in the form of collective learning, unfolds wisdom. Interestingly, some say wisdom springs forth from the fountainhead of perfect intuition. Lastly, nuggets of wisdom morph, wither, contradict, and at times offer newer perspectives, and the cycle goes on until intuitive human experience and applied thinking switch modes so rapidly that one cannot discern, but then that would be an idealistic state.

Human Experience

> 'But human experience is usually paradoxical, that means incongruous with the phrases of current talk or even current philosophy.'
>
> —**George Eliot**

I LIKED THE QUOTE by George Eliot because human experience is truly paradoxical and with the passage of time, one has to keep questioning and revalidating the assumptions and the rationales behind those experiences. At times our own thinking could contradict and become completely different from what we started with in the first place. Even in business or at our workplace, the experiences keep evolving and changing dynamically, trying to satisfy essentially people, markets and the entire ecosystem of shareholders and the community at large.

On May 16, 2004, *Bloomberg Businessweek* covered

an article on 'The power of design'. The article was about Kaiser Permanente, the largest not-for-profit healthcare consortium, based in Oakland, California. It was founded in 1945 by industrialist Harry J. Kaiser and physician Sidney Garfield. In 2003, it was going through a long-range-plan exercise to attract more patients and it was also cutting costs. The company thought that it had to replace hundreds of its medical offices and hospitals with expensive, next generation buildings.

But before it did that, it hired IDEO[1], the Palo Alto, California company, which is a pioneer in design, to help them in their endeavor. IDEO engaged Kaiser's nurses, doctors, and facilities managers and teamed them up with IDEO's social scientists, designers, architects, and engineers. As a part of the consulting exercise, they observed patients as they made their way through their medical facilities and at times they played the role of the patients themselves. Together they came up with some surprising insights.

- Checking into the hospital was a nightmare and patients and their families often became annoyed well before seeing a doctor.
- Waiting rooms were uncomfortable.
- Kaiser's doctors and medical assistants sat too far apart.
- Cognitive psychologists pointed out that often young, infirm, old, and especially immigrants visited doctors with a parent or friend and the second person was not

allowed to stay with the patient, leaving the afflicted alienated and anxious.

- Sociologists explained that patients hated Kaiser's examination rooms because they often had to wait alone for upto 20 minutes half-naked, with nothing to do, surrounded by threatening needles.

Result? The long-range planning of replacing clinics and hospitals with new buildings was chucked. Instead, the focus was turned to 'building human experience in existing buildings', huge cost savings, and potentially happier patients.

At times futuristic planning can hurt thinking, because it is based on accumulated sense of how to do business. But lack of planning hurts execution of innovative ideas. There is no sure-shot way of what works. Importantly, when taking a peek into the future, it is extremely important to understand what consumers and customers really want out of your business. The most important question to answer is: 'Will the experience make a difference to the clients?'

Tom and David Kelley[2], published an article in *Harvard Business Review*, December 2012, titled, 'Reclaim Your Creative Confidence'. In the article, they state that students often come to Stanford University's d.school (earlier Hasso Plattner Institute of Design), to develop their creativity. However, soon they realized that the college's job isn't to teach them creativity but to help them rediscover their creative confidence, which is the natural ability to come up with new ideas and have the courage to try them out and describe four fears which hold people back viz., the fear of the messy unknown, fear of being judged, fear of taking the first step, and fear of losing control. What appealed to me is their example on how the fear of the messy known is broken by Prof. Albert Bandura, a world-renowned psychologist and Stanford professor.

In one of his experiments, he helps people conquer life-long snake phobias (Ophidiophobia) by guiding them through a series of increasingly demanding interactions:

- Watch a snake through a two-way mirror.
- Once comfortable, people would watch it through an open door.
- Then they would watch someone else touch it.
- Then they would start touching the snake using a heavy leather glove.
- Finally, in a few hours, they would touch it with their own hands.

Prof. Bandura calls this process 'guided mastery' of experiencing one small success after another. People who went through the exercise not only were cured of the phobia, but also displayed lesser anxiety and relatively greater success in other parts of their lives when they took up potentially challenging activities like horseback riding or public speaking, which they could have been afraid of taking up earlier. Experiments of this nature help people develop confidence in their ability to attain what they set out to do.

Unleashing the power of human experience and creativity makes people think differently and come out of the conservative and traditional mindsets that they usually box themselves into.

Here is another experiment conducted by James M. Patell, Herbert Hoover Professor of Public and Private Management, Stanford Business School. A computer scientist, two engineers, and an MBA student, took the Extreme Affordability class and quickly realized that, working out of suburban California, they wouldn't be able to complete their group research project to design a low-cost incubator for newborn babies in the developing world. So they gathered their luggage and off they went to rural Nepal, where they had first-hand experience of talking to families and doctors. The insight they picked was, 'The babies in gravest danger were those born prematurely in areas far away from hospitals and not *in* the hospitals'.

So, there was no point in designing an incubator for the hospital. Instead, now they had to design an incubator, to keep babies safe and warm when they were far away from doctors. The team ended up designing a miniature sleeping bag with a pouch, which could store special heat containing wax and it was named, 'The Embrace Infant Warmer'. Compared to a traditional incubator, this sleeping bag cost 99 percent lesser and maintained the right temperature for up to six hours without an external power source. The sleeping bag had the potential to save millions of low birth-weight, premature babies.

The design of this incubator was possible because the team studied the local conditions and got a first-hand experience of what it takes to build an incubator.

One of the many things that people don't often fathom is the importance of local knowledge, understanding and the insights that come with it, when they interact with people on the ground. Most American, European, and Asia-Pacific multinationals try replicating themselves by inculcating their core culture (let us say for simplicity's sake, the way they operate and deploy processes, products, and services) into newer developing geographies and provide less space for local ingenuity to thrive, despite the diversity officer sporting a colourful T-shirt slogan—'pervasive inclusiveness and innovation'. This leads to straight-line thinking and people end up following processes to the 'T', and fail to connect the dots of market opportunities and growth. Human experience is built on adaptability of context and adoption of newer products and services, but most corporations seem to go against this cardinal rule and hence struggle. Following the exuberance of human experience provides true insights for next generation, transformative (not incremental, mind you!) products and services.

Obviously one cannot write a chapter on human experience and creativity without a statement from Steve Jobs[3]. Here is one from *Wired* magazine of 1995: 'Creativity is just connecting things. When you ask creative people how they did something, they feel a little guilty because they didn't really do it; they just saw something. It seemed obvious to them after a while. That's because they were able to connect experiences they've had and synthesize new things. And the reason they were able to do that was that they've had more experiences or they have thought more about their experiences than other people. Unfortunately, that's too rare a commodity. A lot of people in our industry haven't had very diverse experiences. So they don't have enough dots to connect, and they end up with very linear solutions without a broad perspective on the problem. The broader one's understanding of human experience, the better design we will have.'

Human experience transcends design and products. From a services standpoint, it touches the core of growth.

When Steve Jobs took his original McIntosh team for its first retreat—a member asked whether they should do market research on what customers want. Jobs replied, 'No! Because customers don't know what they want until we have shown them. Remember what Ford said, "If I had asked customers what they wanted, they would have told me, a faster horse!"' Leapfrogging products for growth needs tremendous instinct and intuition.

At TGC Consulting, we strongly believe that human experience plays a vital role in connecting the 'unsaid expectations and experiences'. Look at it in a different way. When people convey, it is 50 percent body language, 38 percent is the tone of conversation, and only 7 percent is relayed through words. Now without meeting clients face to face, one will not know what they are really looking for. To that extent, one of the stringent metrics that we follow is: How many clients and people did our consultants meet in a given fortnight? Initially I got a lot of resistance from our people saying, 'What if there is no agenda?' I said, 'Go have coffee with them.' They reluctantly agreed and today they have some of the finest relationships with marquee clients who are global MNCs, Indian conglomerates, and PE/VC funded ventures. Now my colleagues reiterate that every time they meet the client, they come back with newer insights. I am glad it has become a religion now within the firm. Steve Jobs said, 'There is a temptation in our networked age to think that ideas can be developed by email and iChat. That is crazy. Creativity comes from spontaneous meetings, from random discussions. You run into someone, you ask what they are doing, you say, "wow", and soon you are cooking up all sorts of ideas.'

In most of our consulting assignments with clients or even when we do leadership search for senior people, I insist that we meet with all the people concerned with the engagement. That offers a totally different perspective. Once, we had a mandate to fulfil the position of a financial controller for a large MNC. The HR head of the company gave us the job specifications and asked us to get started. We requested on meeting with the hiring manager, who was the CFO of the company. The HR head said, 'You have the specs, let us quickly get started and why meet the CFO.' Very reluctantly we started off on the engagement and lined up senior people to meet with the company. Soon, all the interviews concluded and the hiring manager rejected everyone. This time we insisted on meeting with the hiring manager and the HR agreed. In our meeting, it was evident that she was looking for somebody who was both good in detail as well as in strategy. She was looking for somebody who was action-oriented, a thinker, a strategist, an analyst, a controller, an auditor, a process-oriented person with innovative thinking who understood best-in-class practices, somebody who came with a lot of experience, but at a low cost. In a lighter vein, firstly supermen are rare to spot because they are aliens, secondly they fly most of the time, so they are unreachable, and lastly they are very busy saving the world, so they are not available for hiring. We therefore had to subtly convey this message of the non-existent supermen to the hiring manager as well as understand from her what was the most important criteria that she was looking for, which anyway wasn't mentioned in most standard job specifications.

Meeting people face-to-face is the first best option. If not, Skype is the next best. Lastly, a teleconference is the only option. But if it is only emails, then you can kiss the business goodbye.

The Indian Information technology offshoring industry wouldn't have survived if people from both sides of the ocean didn't travel to meet each other as often as they do. Client partners are positioned with the clients to feel the human interface. Project managers visit the clients every 90 days to get a pulse on what they are looking for. The core of Cognizant Technology Solution's (CTS) strategy lies in customer interfacing and human experience. Most vertical and horizontal heads of CTS are based in the US and sit half a block away from the customer. One senior CTS person told me, 'When the CIO of say Chase wants to meet; we reach him physically within fifteen minutes.

That helps us close deals faster than any other information technology company. We are available, *face-to-face*!'

People who understand human experience and then are able to creatively design solutions usually end up with innovative products and services, which shake up markets and pave way for a larger economic impact. These are the people who are most recognized by companies. Often CEOs of most companies will know their product management specialists, technology architects, and domain specialists by their first name. These people are put in the 'critical human capital' bracket by HR departments and often these people are paid well and taken good care of. For these people the challenge of creating a product or a service, far outweighs any other factor because they derive a sense of satisfaction from having created something of significant value to the company.

The entire social media industry, which has taken the world by a storm in the last decade, has been built on human experience. The personality of Internet changed overnight from a network of connecting people to searching for information to sharing information seamlessly on a real-time basis. In five years, from $272 million annual revenue in 2008, Facebook has jumped to becoming a $5.09 billion social media giant, connecting 1.06 billion monthly active users globally.

Rebecca Van Dyck[6] currently heads consumer marketing at Facebook. She has run the 'Just Do It' campaign globally, launched the iPhone and iPad at Apple, spearheaded the 'Go Forth Campaign' which was Levi's' first global brand identity programme. Citing her trip to Zimbabwe and Rwanda, she says, 'I like to go to places where I have to challenge myself.' Her experience in seeing AIDS or malaria exhausting the communities in Africa, has led her to deeply think of Facebook as a communication tool to solve social problems globally. She adds, 'If someone were to give me a statistic or a data point, I take the other point of view or angle.' That is what experiencing human emotions does to people, changes them to think about alternative and creative viewpoints, and expands the horizons of delivering impact.

More solutions are changing the way people come together to create a new regulation. In November 2009, Michael Migliozzi[7], managing partner at the Los Angles Ad agency, Forza Migliozzi, one day came across an advertisement in *New York Post* that Pabst Brewing Co. was up for sale for $300 million. He tweeted, 'Why don't we crowd source this?' Within a week he launched BuyaBeerCompany.com, and within the next 60 days he had $210 million in pledges. What started as a joke, became serious. Then he got a call from the SEC (Securities and Exchange Commission) and went to Philadelphia, because, as per the regulations dating back to 1933–34, only friends, family, or accredited investors could invest in a business. Then he approached congressmen and in November 2011, a bill titled, 'Entrepreneur Access to Capital Act' was introduced and passed in the house with more than 400 votes. On March 27, 2012 Crowd Fund Act by Senators Brown, Merkley, and Michael Benner was passed along with the JOBS Act. It is a different story that in June 2012, billionaire C. Dean Metropoulos purchased Pabst for about $250 million, and as of last year four top brands of the company are on the decline.

It never occurred to people earlier that there is a creative solution in crowd funding until Migliozzi tried, though it started as a joke. Eventually it turned into an act where it helps small entrepreneurs to raise funding to buy and run companies. If we step out of our bounds and try to pursue opportunities or seek to make a change, then people rally in support and then the change is inevitable. Governments change when the communities put pressure; and communities are influenced by people, who want to step out of their comfort zones to create better human experiences for the collective good.

In 1892, Asa Griggs Candler incorporated Coca Cola Company. In 1915, Harold Hirsch, an attorney of the company, came up with a suggestion of launching a national competition to design a bottle, which will distinguish it from its rivals. The brief given was, 'A bottle which a person could recognize even if they felt it in the dark, and so shaped that even if broken, a person could tell at a glance, what it was.' Coca Cola essentially focused on two things—creating a human experience and creating a brand. Inspired by the cocoa pod that he came across in the encyclopedia at the Emeline Fairbanks Memorial library, Earl R. Dean of Root Glass Company of Terre Haute, Indiana, made a sketch and subsequently the prototype of the famous countered Coca Cola bottle, and sent it to win the competition. Interestingly, the original counter's diameter was larger than the bottom, thereby making the bottle unstable for production, which then was improvised and the world famous Coca Cola bottle was born with the diameter of the bottom and the counter being the same.

Inspiration and connecting the dots often enhance human experience! Some call it common sense or making sense of patterns.

Common Sense

'The three great essentials to achieve anything worthwhile are, first, hard work; second, stick-to-itiveness; third, common sense.'

—Thomas A. Edison

I BELIEVE COMMON SENSE is about applying simple rationality in the given current social, business, or economic context. Essentially it lies in doing the best in a given context and there are no specific formulae. Aristotle defined common sense as the actual power of inner sensation as opposed to judgement arising from the five senses (seeing, touching, smelling, tasting, and hearing). Merriam Webster dictionary defines common sense as: 'Sound and prudent judgement based on a simple perception of the situation or facts.' Now let us look at some real life incidents and examples.

This one is hilarious. My brother, who lives in the US, told me an interesting story. Apparently once, a robber entered a wine store, swung his pistol out, and shouted at the cashier to part with all the cash in the register. The scared lady quickly took out all the cash and put it on the desk for the robber to take it with him. The robber quickly stashed the cash into his bag and while going, he decided to grab a few bottles of wine. As he picked his wine, the cashier timidly said, 'Wine can be picked only if you are above eighteen years of age,' to which the robber smiled and flashed his ID card saying that he was above eighteen and left. The young lady promptly called the cops with the identification and the robber was caught! Sometimes having a good presence of mind can be termed as common sense.

In mid 1800s, California was under the grip of a gold rush. About 3,00,000 miners arrived at Sutter's mill in Sierra Nevada, and nearly $43 million a year of gold was being mined, mostly by Wells Fargo. Levi Strauss[5] and his brother-in-law David Stern noticed that these thousands of miners needed fabric, scissors, blankets, buttons, and canvas cloth. So, together, they opened a wholesale shop to supply to various stores in west US. Levi applied common sense and also sold to the miners directly carrying merchandise on a horseback. During interactions with the miners, they told him that the cotton britches tore and gold ore spilled from their pockets. So he got into manufacturing of trousers from canvas sail cloth with sturdy pockets, which wouldn't split. Soon he ran out of canvas, so Levi ordered sturdier fabric named Serge DeNimes, a material named after the city in south of France. Soon the name was shortened to Denim. Around 1872, a tailor, Jacob Davis invented the process of sewing metal rivets into the men's work trousers, at points of strain, where it tore the most. Since he was short of funds, Jacob approached Levi to patent the process together and US patent 1,39,121 was issued for placing copper rivets in men's pants. As you can see a series of events led one to the other and Levi's blue jeans was born. Was it strategic thinking? Definitely not. Was it serendipity? Not really! Levi used his common sense to identify an opportunity and went about fulfilling it.

Common sense, at times, is identifying the opportunity at hand, and trying to fulfil it. And there are many opportunities out there. We often reject what we ought to pursue, even before an idea is fully born. Only those who unlock the power behind common sense, actually get there.

With minimal support and upon strong insistence from senior management, I took up the assignment of starting a new business unit. The client was excruciatingly painful and the pricing for the engagement was so ridiculously low that life became hell to generate even miniscule margins. To achieve reasonable gross margins, we had to be stringent with budgets and the compensation offered was below market rates. So we ended up recruiting those we could afford and fortunately we could see a few sparks of talent here and there. But then, most were rookies. The rookies needed time to mature, couldn't handle the deliverables on the go, and managers came under intense pressure, and the client started crying foul. After the first few months into this business, several times, I vehemently opposed doing business with the client and expressed that we were working with the wrong client both from a pricing and attitude point of view, and our efforts do not justify the returns. But the management anticipated large volumes of business from the client and insisted that we continue to plod away. But in reality the client had no intention of giving any large volume business. In fact, the client exactly knew our predicament. Sitting on a high pedestal, the client turned ruthless. Partnering really never mattered and the client was continually playing one vendor against the other for want of better pricing. Reduction in pricing was a topic of discussion in every agenda and meeting; and I often felt like a freshman under the scanner. It was like a pressure cooker, ready to burst anytime. Soon things became unbearable, employees stopped smiling, the joining ratio plummeted, attrition started to climb, and though we were making some margins, we were sucking the system dry and none of us were happy.

Every coin always has two sides—the client continued

to gain from the abysmally low price, and the management from additional revenues—and we were being flipped in between. But then such environments don't last long and this too ended pretty quickly. Personally, it was an eye opener. Very early on, I was fortunate enough to get a deeper understanding of people and what their real motivations were, and I moved on to the next assignment. The management too learnt its lessons and in the meanwhile engagement with the client concluded. After all, we are humans and have our desires and beliefs despite everything that we come by in our lives.

Prejudices and emotions often create a veil and suppress common sense from surfacing. It is utter common sense not to work with clients, from whom many stalwarts already walked away, and it is a pity that we didn't learn from other's experiences. But then, often common sense unfolds only after all the mistakes have been made and one relegates the past to oblivion. The experience unshackled my thinking and fresher horizons dawned, which otherwise wouldn't have. In retrospect, after working with global organizations and world-class managements, though it is common sense, the insights I gained were significant viz., 'Work with clients who value your contribution, who do not commoditize your worth by offering peanuts. Secondly, it is a futile proposition to provide a discount upfront in anticipation of future volumes. Discounting should be scaled on realization of volumes. Who knows, in the years to come, managements might change, contracts could be rescaled, and monkeys could fly. Thirdly, one should always work only with world-class managements who have the propensity to listen, learn, and adapt. Lastly, heed to common sense and listen to others when it comes to understanding people and their motives but rely on your inner voice.'

Uncle Tom's Cabin was one my favourite childhood novels. It is a heart-rendering piece of work depicting the life of African–American slaves. The author of this book, Harriet Beecher Stove said, 'Common sense is seeing things as they are; and doing things as they ought to be.'

Donald Petersen was the CEO of Ford from 1985–1990. During one of his visits to the Ford Design Centre, to review the new Thunderbird designs, he looked at the faces of the designers and asked them, 'Is this the car you would like to drive and park in your driveway?' After a few moments of hesitation, Ford's chief design executive, Jack Telnack answered frankly, 'Absolutely not, I wouldn't want the car to be parked in my driveway.' After further questioning and probing, it became evident that the designers were just following what the management wanted to see, which was an incremental design over the previous year's car models. Petersen then told the designers to recreate the designs and went ahead and invested nearly $3.2 billion in the design, architecture, and launch of jelly bean shaped cars. Hence, the Taurus and Mercury Sable twins were born, and these models gave Ford a resurgent outlook for sales and pushed it forward to the next decade.

Common sense is about asking the right questions and helping people achieve their highest potential. If we don't let designers think, managers execute, and leaders show a vision—how can the world move forward? Stifling away the energies of thinking and execution takes the wind off the breath of people's motivation.

Dakin Sloss[2], president of CACS, blogged in August 2011, in *Huffington Post*: 'Looking at poor budgeting and inefficient bureaucracy by the state government of California, and the declining standards of education at schools and rising cost of living, a group of Stanford students and alumni came together to start California Common Sense (CACS), a Stanford based non-profit group. The concept was simple—'Knowledge is power, combine Silicon Valley's technology prowess with the analytical abilities of Stanford University'. They decided to open government records, analyse data, and present how the budgets could work better. So as a first step, they mapped the hierarchy of the 3,800 plus state agencies, councils, committees, sections, and departments, and created online maps. And what they found was that the functions of many of these departments overlapped. For example, the Bureau of Gambling Control and Gambling Control Commission had almost similar functions and both were getting funded. Some other interesting data they found include lifeguards in California were being paid $57,646 on an average compared to $28,004 in other states. Despite reordering prison population due to bad living conditions in the state prisons, the correctional department spent $246.50 per resident of the state compared to an average of $157.60 for other states. California's legislative branch paid $1.75 a page to print legislation in 2007 and given modern technology, bills do not need to be printed, or should only cost 10 cents per page.

It is common sense that most governments at different levels (national, state, and municipal) around the world are less efficient and more bureaucratic in managing budgets and spending the taxpayer money. But somehow none look at it from a structural standpoint and involve knowledge centers for effective deployment of resources. Common sense says that transparency and ceding power in deployment of state resources creates bureaucratic disequilibrium and hence the resistance will be large. Common sense says that large bodies need to be dissected and smaller bodies integrated, and somewhere in between is the right balance.

Warren Buffet[3], one of the world's richest people, had a simple idea for investing—identify cheap stock relative to its potential value, a simple business any person with decent potential should be able to run, invest in volume, wait for the price to go up, sell, or acquire, split and move on. He says, when investing, he applies common sense to his judgment. When he comes across interesting products in supermarts, he looks at the details of the company and analyses the strengths and invests. He looks beyond the revenues, income, PE ratios, invest-debt ratios etc. He looks at products, services, and people behind the business and invests. Stepping back and looking at his methodology, one would say it is sheer common sense. However, I have always felt that common sense comes with a deep understanding of data, pattern recognition, and the ability to see the future through the maze of information.

In another interesting incident, Buffet was playing golf with his close friends at Pebble beach California and the friends wagered a bet that if Buffet made a hole in one, he would be paid $20,000 and if he didn't, he would have to pay them $10. In a lopsided bet of this nature, though bleak, often people look at the possibility of making exceedingly high returns and go for the bet. Warren asked a simple question: 'What is the probability of my winning?' and he came to know that his chances were near zero and he didn't take the bet. Why lose $10, when you know for sure that you aren't going to make it. Common sense is about properly weighing risks in the context of rational thought and not getting entangled with the attainment of improbabilities.

Dr Edwin M. Glasscock[3] writes an interesting story in his book, *Common Sense #1 Critical Success Factor*, 'Verne Willaman started his career as a sales representative and finished as the member of the executive committee of Johnson & Johnson. When asked the reason for his success, he replied that he hired good people and he followed a simple process. He would interview the first time, then ask for a second round, then have a few more rounds of pacing, check references, and finally ask himself the question, "Would I like to go on a cruise with this person for three weeks?" If the answer to this gut level question were negative, then he wouldn't hire the person.'

It is simple common sense that when hiring a person, you should like the person and would want to spend time with that person. Often people make the mistake of hiring for skills. But then, if you are going to spend a substantial portion of your life with that person, then look for attitude and comfort level as well. Simple rules like this help make better business decisions and life can be far more easier.

After the Second World War, to contend with the spread of communism, state department officials William L. Clayton and George F. Kennan came up with the economic support plan for the reconstruction of war-torn European nations. Secretary of State, George Marshall, spoke extensively about the reconstruction plan at Harvard as a part of the War Reconstruction Efforts Seminar. During 1947–51, the US Government spent $13 billion of economic assistance to help in the recovery of European nations that participated in the Organization for European Economic Cooperation. The investment was almost 5 percent of US' GDP of $248 billion in 1948. In fact, the US spent an additional 5 percent even before the Marshall plan came into force towards reconstruction efforts. The story goes that the planners wanted to name it the 'Truman Plan' and suggested so to the president. But Truman sensed that Congress might reject the idea if his name was attached with the plan and suggested that the plan should be named after the secretary of state and hence it ended up being known as the Marshall plan. Truman applied a simple judgement, more of a common sense, that it was possible that political thought might overpower the concept of the plan, which was extremely important for the development of a free world. Leadership and common sense are often strongly related because leaders seem to see through the consequences of actions much better than the others.

Dr Greenstein, professor of politics at Princeton University, wrote in *History News Network* in July 2002, 'Eisenhower had a temper that could burst forth like a summer thunderstorm, but that subsided just as rapidly. He also had a quality that has come to be called "emotional intelligence", the ability to turn one's feelings to constructive purposes and prevent them from impeding the performance of one's responsibilities.' Apparently, when Eisenhower was angry, instead of yelling at the person he was angry with, he would write a long letter and kept it in his drawer. After ten days, he would review the letter, in a better emotional state of mind, and then decide whether to pass it along or throw it in the dustbin. Many of us know that lack of understanding our emotions and self-control leads to disastrous effects. We also know that simple methods and common sense helps resolve many issues, but we hardly take a step back and try to resolve our inner conflicts, before resolving any external conflicts. It is common sense to understand what ticks and what doesn't!

During my early years in management, once, a senior executive of the company asked for feedback and with all sincerity, I poured it out to him in good faith. Initially, I hesitated, but upon his insistence, I decided to be truthful and told him politely that he was far too transactional and was missing the forest for the trees and had to work on his transformational expertise. His lips quivered, his face contorted, his eyebrows twitched, and he asked for data-points, which I listed for him systematically and explained where he was messing things up and why people didn't really feel he was a leader. I also put it in an even tone that his understanding of global culture and nuances relating to etiquette needed significant improvement. Boom! Within the next ten minutes, I knew that I blew it. It is common sense not to give such candid straight talk to senior executives. They have fragile egos and feedback of this nature can be devastating. There is a right time, right place, and must importantly a right way to give feedback to senior people. I was possibly like a bull in a china shop. After that, for a few weeks, he exchanged uncomfortable smiles. Finally, one day, I said, 'I am sorry if I have been way too forthright, and perhaps its uncomfortable and probably I should leave the company?' He just smiled and I felt a bit relieved, not fully though, and after that session, we couldn't develop a strong relationship. Once the thin armour of ego is pierced, it becomes very difficult and time-consuming to rebuild it. One has to be extremely careful, ideally, be diplomatic in such sensitive situations, and convey the message in such a way that the concerned person gets the point and at the same time is not offended.

Perhaps it is an art to achieve that, but I guess seasoned professionals master this art of giving powerful feedback with subtlety.

Common sense is being sensible—what to say, when to say, what not to say, and how to say. Research says that, 'How you say it matters more than what you say—to determine success' (HBR, April 2012).

In India, there is a website named ipaidabribe.com—where people write stories of where, when, and why they paid a bribe. Most cases reported are when people go to government offices—land registration, vehicle registration, when they go to the police for help, when people need any kind of certificate, and such others. Even a high school kid knows the points of corruption. The financials of corruption in the political and bureaucratic class is staggering with most publicly noted scams being in the range of $1–5 billion. In April 2013, *Times of India* reported that for many MLAs, increase in wealth over a five year term was a staggering 10,000 percent. Incidentally, their salaries are in the range of $50,000 per annum and their net worth was upwards of $10–20 million. The problem of corruption is something everybody knows, but nobody seems to know how to tackle ait. Common sense says: just act and be done with it! Between 2010–2012 social activists waged hunger strikes, new political parties spawned up with the motto to fight corruption, millions of people took to streets, social networking sites recorded more than a billion messages and tweets on the subject of corruption—but then, soon all of this whittled out. The energy generated was trying to attempt a systemic change, where the whole machinery was expected to act by itself and self-destruct, which obviously was not going to happen. While every nation churns its wheels on governance, structure, processes, and systems, the real nation runs because of the fundamental values that govern human behaviour. Ideally, systemic change comes from change in individual behaviours. Education helps to an extent, awareness about social problems plaguing the society also does its part, but it is the change in people's mindset, which is going to bring about the desired results. The former president of India, Dr APJ Abdul Kalam said, 'I believe only parents can bring about that change by being role models', which, when you give it a deep thought, is perhaps the best viable solution. Takes longer, but results will sustain. Utter common sense is to first fix the problem at home. People cannot live two lives—one at home and the other outside, usually behaviours converge and responsible citizenship has to start from home.

Unusual, but common sense doesn't seem to be nurtured as much in homes, schools, and offices. Somehow people don't seem to question, and blindly follow existing patterns, and that seems to be the norm. A few decades back, before the advent of mobile phones, people rented phones from AT&T for a fee and took the instruments with them when they moved. AT&T called upon McKinsey[1] to figure out a way to help find a method to prevent the disappearance of phones. McKinsey's finding was classic. 'The cost of trying to recover the phones was more than the cost of phones itself'. Questioning the problem often yields a different kind of result.

Intuition

'Intuition is seeing with the soul.'

—**Dean Koontz**

THE DICTIONARY MEANING OF intuition is: The act or faculty of knowing or sensing without the use of rational processes, a sense of immediate cognition. Knowledge gained by the use of this faculty, a perceptive insight and a sense of something not evident or deducible; kind of an impression.

Jack Welch, former CEO of GE, stated in his book *Winning*: 'Sometimes making a decision is hard not because it is unpopular, but because it comes from the gut and defies a "technical" rationale. Much has been written about the mystery of gut, but it's really just pattern recognition, isn't it. You've seen something so many times you just know what's going on this time. The facts may be incomplete or the data limited, but the situation feels very, very familiar to you.'

I had the opportunity to engage with three interesting CEOs with very different styles of working and all the three learnt and looked at the same situation in very distinct ways. With one person, reams of data, notes, and discussions preceded any decision and at times decisions got delayed and sometimes not taken too, especially when data was not coherent enough or when the notes didn't precede the meeting. Eventually when the decision was taken, it was an extrapolation of the data at hand. When this person went for negotiations, he took along with him predominantly excel spreadsheets and very little cognizance was given to human emotion. Each meeting was a marathon meeting covering miniscule details and lasted for hours at a stretch. But then, many decisions this person took were right and many weren't. I am not trying to disparage any style, but just trying to make a point, that this CEO learnt and executed by 'reading and discussing' and he is a highly successful CEO.

Peter Drucker[1,2,3], in his seminal article on management in HBR writes, 'During the Second World War, when Eisenhower was the commander of the Allied Forces in Europe, the press loved him for his brilliant answers. A decade later, during his presidency, the press ate him alive for his incoherent answers.' What happened? When he was a commander, the questions had to be submitted in writing before the conference his aides prepared, and he read them extensively before he went to meet the press. During his presidency, none of that happened, he answered questions on the fly and things didn't work out. He was a reader.

The second CEO I engaged with would write copious notes from meetings with customers, employees, partners, and stakeholders and would detail out problems and opportunities at hand. He maintained notes on all his thoughts and what was expected from each person he met from time to time. He would go into meetings with copious notes, fall back on them from time to time, and during negotiations, he would again write notes, reiterate what was said, and take decisions based on the notes he prepared. Often his meetings lasted for couple of hours and many of the decisions he took were right and a few weren't. He learnt and executed by 'writing and doing pre-analysis'. Again, he was a successful CEO.

Similarly, Winston Churchill would spend hours writing notes and crafting the intricacies of all his major speeches. His friend Lord Birkenhead said, 'Winston has spent the best years of his life writing impromptu speeches.' Beethoven made notes copiously, which he never referred to while composing. He said, 'If I don't write it down, I forget, but I write it, I don't forget, but don't have to look up.' Both of them learnt and executed by 'writing'. All these people seem to have developed their habits intuitively, based on what works for them and what doesn't.

The third CEO would, however, come into the meeting and just ask the right questions, review the presentations in real-time, listen intently, grasp the opportunities and problems at hand, and make decisions on the fly. An hour before any negotiation, he would call his senior team to a room, close his eyes, and intently listen as the executives poured it out for him and he would then debate the pros and cons. He was not overtly concerned with data at hand, but how to make the negotiations work so as to make a larger business impact from the deal. Again this CEO made many more decisions, which went the right way and few obviously didn't work out. This CEO made decisions from his gut and said that he often relied on intuition. This CEO learnt and executed based on 'intuitive understanding and listening'.

Franklin D. Roosevelt, Harry Truman, Lyndon Johnson—all these American presidents were listeners and enjoyed free-flowing press conferences. John F. Kennedy was a reader and he had a staff of many writers. Some of them took decisions intuitively and some based their decisions on non-intuitive alternatives.

When I reflect, the decisions taken by the third CEO were perhaps as good and if not better compared to the decisions taken by the first two CEOs. There is no clear rationale to how intuition works, but he consumed far less management time, spent far lesser effort to take decisions, and was as successful as the first two. It is more likely that maturity and experience adds to better our intuitions, probably a different dimension to pattern recognition, for better decision-making.

Intuition is that sense which, if developed well, has the ability to cut through the layers of information on hand and lets you know the decision you ought to be taking and at times even without considering the information at hand. Then it is left for the individual to decide whether to go by it or pursue some other path. Often, senior executives tell me that when they took decisions based on intuition, it works far better, but all of them clearly reiterate that they look at data, often rely on intuition, and are open to taking a contrarian view compared to the non-intuitive alternatives at hand.

During his Nobel Laureate lecture, world famous psychologist, Daniel Kahneman[5] identified two ways of thinking. Intuitive thinking is perception-like, rapid, effortless, fast, automatic, emotional, and associative. In contrast, deliberate thinking is reasoning-like, critical, analytic, rule-governed, flexible, slow, serial, and neutral. Interestingly, most judgments and actions are governed in the intuitive mode. When you are driving a car, initially you struggle, but eventually intuitive driving takes over and you listen to the radio as you drive and you are on autopilot mode, not really thinking hard as you drive. Likewise experienced writers effortlessly string words to articulate their proposition and it happens without the conscious mind applying itself. The non-conscious mind takes control and experienced artists draw right from the heart, and the conscious mind, at times, looks at how their drawing is taking shape as their hands move in rapid strokes. Some behavioural scientists call this 'entering the zone'.

With the explosion of data and with algorithmic analytics-based logic giving deeper insights, corporate executives and social scientists will perhaps have a better understanding of human behaviour and emotions beneath them. But possibly analytics cannot replace intuition because intuition arises from making consciousness kinetic, a sense which is beyond the physical faculties. Intuition perhaps is the ability to dig into the recesses of the mind, combining it with the cues that nature offers, and coming out with a real-time directive. Often people say that 'in a flash, it occurred to me.' What does it mean? It means that for a flash of a moment the brain opened up a new, dimension and people got a conscious peek into a higher form of intelligence, where the information entropy is nil, which means the measure of unpredictability reaches absolute certainty even in measuring random variables and it is also called non-conscious decision making. This kind of decision-making arrives at a solution without even the relevance of a question, because information processing or questioning is a binary or an approach towards multi-variant choice making.

Prof. Andrew Wiles, mathematician and professor at Princeton, solved the required proof of Fermat's last theorem, which for 358 years was an unsolved puzzle. In early 1993, he presented proof at a conference in Cambridge, but by August 1993, other mathematicians found a gap, and as he was trying to bridge the gap, he realized that his error was significant. He spent agonizing hours trying to solve it, because somewhere he knew that he was close to it, but the proof was elusive. On September 19, 1994, Wiles had an insight—a flash that he had to go back to an earlier approach that he had abandoned earlier. Within five days, he submitted the manuscript and in May 1995, it was published in *Annals of Mathematics*. That is the non-conscious brain solving a problem, being at it, even when the conscious brain is pursuing some other activity. For those who are curious, Fermat's theorem is simple to read, it states that no three positive integers a, b, and c can satisfy the equation $a^n + b^n = c^n$ for any integer value of n greater tematicshan two. Here is a trivia: When Prof. Wiles was 10 years old, he came across this theorem in the local library. He found the statement of the theorem easy to understand, but hard to solve due to his rudimentary understanding of math then, but importantly, he made a decision to be the first person to solve it.

During his early years, in 1956, working as Professor at MIT, Amar Gopal Bose[7] bought a high-end stereo speaker system, but was disappointed with the speakers, which failed to reproduce good quality sound. This motivated him to conduct extensive research on speaker technology and that led him to invent the stereo loudspeaker. His focus on psychoacoustics led him to design speakers for a home setting, with specific emphasis on reflective sound, similar to the sound-field perceived by listeners in a classical concert hall. Bose said that ideas come to him as a flash, 'These innovations are not the result of rational thought; it's an intuitive idea.' Amar Bose is the founder of nearly $2.5 billion worth Bose Corporation with about 10,000 employees worldwide.

The paradox is that John Gertner in his book *Idea Factory*, about innovation at Bell Labs writes, 'We usually imagine that invention occurs in a flash, with a eureka moment that leads a lone inventor towards a startling epiphany. In truth, large leaps in technology rarely have a precise point of origin. At the start, forces that precede an invention merely begin to align, often imperceptibly, as a group of people and ideas converge, until over the course of months or years or decades, they gain clarity and momentum and the help of additional ideas and actors. Luck seems to matter and so does timing for it tends to be the case that the right answers, the right people, the right place—perhaps all three—require a serendipitous encounter with the right problem. And then, sometimes, a lead. Only in retrospect do such leaps look obvious.' When Niels Bohr, along with Einstein, the world's greatest physicist, heard in 1938 that splitting a uranium atom could yield a tremendous burst of energy, he slapped his head and said, 'Oh, what idiots we have all been.'

Intelligence of the highest order conveys a decision indeterminate of the data available. If you notice carefully, often, true experiences of intuition align with singularity, because all other choices tend to block out momentarily. Besides choosing from more alternatives means higher information entropy and that is lower order intelligence. But let us not confuse intuition with unconfirmed decision-making, arising out of prejudiced judgmental confidence that people often make based on their past experiences. 'While intuition can provide with unusual insights, at times it can dangerously mislead,' says David G. Myers, professor of psychology, Hope College, US.

Quoting Bob Woodward, from *Bush at War*, George W. Bush said, 'I am a gut player, I rely on my instinct,' before launching the Iraq war. That is the peril of following intuition, at least perceived intuition. Perception is a form of intuition, and people, based on their perceptions, could go right or wrong in their judgement, just like people might go awry taking decisions based on conscious, rational thinking. There is a thin line between intuition and preferential confidence, a fuzzy extrapolation of interpretation of non-intuitive alternatives, and one has to be extremely careful. Prof. Adrian Furnham[6], professor of psychology at University of London says that people may at times depend on heuristics—mental shortcuts that allow us to make judgements quickly and efficiently. These rules of thumb are similar to intuitions; they allow us to function without constantly stopping to think through problems from first principles. The problem is that while heuristics can be helpful they can also lead to errors.

Again, perception of ordinary day-to-day events, which is judgemental, rapid, and experiential, is akin to intuition, depending upon the situation, though impressionably a lower level of intuition compared to the 'aha', big breakthrough kind of intuition. This makes me believe that there are gradual levels in the non-conscious form of cognition, starting from simplistic impressions, experiences, pattern making to creation of new ideas or solving complex problems or puzzles or theorems. And seems like, one can, with maturity and experience and continual hard work, hone the power of intuition. Physical systems can be worked upon to get desired results from cognition and vice versa.

This has been a revelation and psychologists world over are working upon some ground-breaking theories.

A study published in the August 2006 issue of the *Journal of Experimental Psychology: General*, explains why people are predisposed to trusting their intuitions even when presented with information that suggests that their intuition may be wrong. The study conducted by Joseph Simmons of the Yale School of Management and Leif Nelson of New York University, shows that people frequently choose an intuitive option over an equally good non-intuitive alternative because often people hold their intuition with confidence. This confidence makes them believe that their intuitions are accurate and hence, should be followed, despite other non-intuitive choices at hand. However, when it is hard to generate an intuition, people often decide to give more consideration to the alternatives. For example, when people favour a political candidate based on intuition, it is more likely for them to stick to the candidate, despite being presented with flaws. But then, it is feasible for people to choose non-intuitive choices with persuasive messages.

Then there is Prof. Myer's lecture about Japanese chick sexers. What is it? It is the ability of a person to identify the sex of the chick within a few days of birth. Now, why is chicken sexing important? Usually it takes 30 days for an average person to notice the sex of chicken and it takes an average of 200 days from birth for a chicken to lay a decent sized egg of about 60 grams (2 ounces). So if there is a segregation of sexes at birth, or within a few days of birth, two separate programmes can be run. One for the hens, where they are fed (about 100 grams of feed a day), nourished, kept warm, and cared for, and second for the males. Usually the males are culled or some retained for meat. So if the sexing takes longer, the cost incurred in feeding millions of males doesn't justify the cost of the egg for arriving at a competitive market pricing. In Japan, chick sexers are trained for 5 months on how to determine the sex of a chicken and for the students to get certified, a test is conducted once every six months, where they have to segregate 400 chicks in 36 minutes with 99 percent accuracy for females and 97 percent accuracy for males. Usually it takes three years to master the skill and to clear the test. However, in commercial farms, the expected accuracy is usually closer to 95 percent. Usually Japanese students take up this course to migrate to Europe and US, where they earn as high as $1,00,000 per annum and are regarded as assets with specialized skills. With such extensive training and years of experience, Japanese chick sexers are able to recognize the sex of a one-day-old chicken compared to their American counterparts.

The Japanese experts were able to do it because they intuitively develop the ability to see patterns, a skill which comes with maturity and experience. So the Americans were sent to Japan on apprenticeship to learn how these people train and how they understand patterns intuitively, because one cannot write manuals about human intuitive understanding of patterns. The transfer of such knowledge is through human intuitive transference which one gets when they soak in that ecosystem.

He further explains that vision operates as two different systems—the conscious perception and the intuitive programme. The British Psychological Society published an article by a blind-sight researcher about how the retina transfers information to the visual cortex and also to other areas of the brain. So, if the visual cortex is damaged, then the person is blind-sighted, which means consciously she cannot see, but intuitively responds to various situations. University of St Andrews conducted an experiment on a person who is blind-sighted, and held a pencil in front of that person in different angles and she couldn't obviously see. But when asked to grab the pencil, she exactly reached out at the correct angle to grab the pencil. Similarly she could post an envelope in a mail slot with varying angles with great accuracy. So that is the power of intuitive information processing.

Clarence Saunders opened Piggly Wiggly stores in 1916 in Memphis, Tennessee, and quickly understood that it was commercially more viable to start a self-service model where customers could pick from the aisles, instead of relying on counter boys. Saunders purchased in wholesale, at night weighed and measured and placed the merchandise on the shelves, and in the morning consumers picked them quickly. This helped in the lowering of prices and enhanced profits. He was awarded several patents for introducing this novel method and Piggly Wiggly chain grew rapidly with franchising. Soon this inspired many stores to start self-service and Kroger Stores, Herrin, Illinois was one, where Michael J. Cullen worked as the sales manager. Cullen intuitively came up with the idea of self-service supermarkets instead of multiple smaller grocery stores and in 1929 wrote to the president of Krogers to adapt a new strategy of opening supermarkets which could be ten times more profitable. But a subordinate of the president quashed the idea. Cullen, meanwhile, made up his mind, and in 1930 moved with his family to Long Island and along with a friend, leased a 6000 sq. ft abandoned garage in Jamaica Avenue in the suburbs of Queens. The store was called 'King Kullen' with the tag line, 'Pile it High. Sell it Low' and opened operations on August 4, 1930. By 1935, seventeen 'King Kullen' super markets were making revenues of $6 million. With revenues of close to $1 billion, and as per *Supermarket News*, 'King Kullen' is regarded as 'Americas 75 North American Food Retailers'.

Probably for Kullen it could have been a dash of intuition or perhaps a calculated decision, nobody really knows. But calculation at the time of planning often doesn't stack up to reality, as it unfolds later. A judicious mix of intuition, faith in oneself, and calculated risk probably helps build large enterprises.

Grand chessmasters like Viswanathan Anand[4], Garry Kasparov, Anatoly Karpov, and Emanuel Lasker remember as many as 50,000 or more chess board formations and with a glance on the chessboard, they can intuitively know how the game could end. For a novice chess player, it is reasoning and analysis at every step. But for a grandmaster, it is intuitive understanding of patterns, something that the mind tunes to very comfortably. At times, deep expertise induces intuitive pattern understanding and it comes with its own pros and cons. While patterns can tell you a story based on existing experience, patterns could also mislead, because patterns often again result in making choices, which is conscious decision-making and the entropy is higher. It is a thin line and one has to decide. Each one to themselves, as they say!

Another view could be that intuitiveness is always in cohorts with non-intuitive choices, and awakens only when entropy is high and the observer is unable to decide. But then, that could be prejudiced. Duality applies, observer influences the observation and vice versa, which means conscious alternatives influence intuition and vice versa. In such cases predictive modeling of decisions is impossible to align with a singular output, until the outcomes are pre-decided, which often may not be the case in real world applications and systems.

The idea behind this chapter was to gain insights into the world of the non-conscious, an autopilot we all run on, and the importance of conscious, critical thinking, or perhaps a combination of the two.

Leap of Faith

> 'There are many talented people who haven't fulfilled their dreams because they over thought it, or they were too cautious, and were unwilling to make the leap of faith.'
>
> —**James Cameron**

AT THE AGE OF 17, in 1919, Allen Lane Williams[2] joined as an apprentice at Bodley Head, a publishing house, founded by his uncle John Lane. He quickly rose in ranks and in 1925, following the death of his uncle became the managing editor of the company. Allen Lane was overtly forthright by nature and was often at loggerheads with the board on what to publish and what to market. When James Joyce's controversial book Ulysses was published, the board had serious issues with Allen Lane, and he left the company. Sometime in 1934, Lane visited Agatha

Christie and on his return, at Exeter station platform, was feeling frustrated with nothing affordable available, worth reading. Then he looked around at the bored faces of fellow travellers as they waited endlessly on the platforms for trains to arrive. He had an idea. He conceived the paperback editions of literature with proven quality and cheap enough for people to buy them from vending machines, just the way people bought cigarettes. The first book vending machine, 'Penguincubator', was set at Charing Cross Road. He wanted to take the books from libraries and traditional bookshops to streets, railway stations, bus stops, shopping areas, where people could buy from anywhere. His concept was simple; books were another medium of entertainment that people could indulge in, while they went about pursuing whatever they were doing.

The genesis of his paperback idea, to an extent, was influenced from the concept of paperback for the mass market introduced by the German publisher Albatross books, which had an Albatross as its logo, and the company couldn't take off.

Evidently paperbacks have existed for a long time since 1900s in the form of pamphlets, pornographic books, foreign editions, banned books, and railway books. Lane introduced affordable, good quality books into this segment. When Lane started the company, he named it after the grounded Penguin for its visibility and strength.

A logo was prominently displayed on the cover and the genre was colour coded on the covers—dark blue for biographies, green for crime, and orange for fiction.

Soon the books took off and the logo became synonymous with affordable paperback. Eminent authors and contemporary publishers took cognizance of the market impact that the product created and started supporting it. Book shops and libraries, which until then were buying only hard, bounds at six to eight shillings, soon started ordering paperbacks, which were much cheaper at six pence. The first Penguin author list consisted of contemporary authors—Andre Maurois, Ernst Hemingway, Beverly Nichols, Mary Webb, Norman Doughlas, and E. Arnot Robinson. Lane placed large print orders and persuaded non-literary retailers to stock the books.

Within the first ten months, Lane had printed 1 million paperbacks with the book *Ariel* by Andre Maurois becoming the bestseller. In 1937, Penguin imprints covering contemporary issues, was launched. Soon Penguin became a world-renowned name. In 1952, Allen Lane was knighted.

The venture proved extremely successful and in 1940, he expanded into Puffin Books and in 1945 Penguin Classics was born. On November 3, 1960, Penguin published D.H. Lawrence's *Lady Chatterley's Lover*, one of the bestselling and most lucrative books from Penguin's stable.

Sometime in 1965, the chief editor, Tony Godwin and the board decided to get rid of Lane for his non-traditional ways and for blocking experimenting with newer covers, designs, and concepts for domestic and international markets. Besides, Godwin and Lane were also having many disagreements and divergence in thoughts. Meanwhile, Lane stole the entire print-run of the French cartoonist Sine, titled *Massacre* and burnt it. Soon after that incident, Lane fired Godwin and retained control of the company. He then introduced hard-bounds, something that he vehemently fought in his earlier days. In 1970, Pearson bought the cash-strapped Penguin, within six weeks after the death of Allen Lane. As on 2013, Penguin and Random House have merged.

Amazon's Kindle, Apple's iBooks, and Google Books are the Penguincubators of the 21st century and distribution seems to have taken over creation of content. Interestingly, Lane addressed both the content and distribution ideas. But publishers somewhere along the way didn't see the landscape of distribution change and now have no option but to either forward, integrate, and create technology platforms that help readers have easy access, which is an expensive proposition, or take the niche way of working on content platforms, while entering into partnerships with technology distributors. This is a classic example of how technology products and services have created a disruption in the reading habits of consumers and have displaced the traditional physical distribution systems of publishers.

If you have an idea, then take a leap of faith and go after it. Churn the seas and do whatever it takes to take the idea to fulfilment. Success comes to those who go after it and not to those who merely talk about it. When I meet people, I can often figure out whether the person is going to do something about it or just flirt with the idea. Those who carry their idea to execution are those who are single-mindedly focussed on creating it and think about how to do it, rather than waste time discussing pros and cons of whether that is something they should pursue or not. A half-baked cake, still in the oven, is never as tasty as a hot chocolate fudge served across the counter. You know when the idea is ripe and when you have to jump in. People who moonshine are often caught between the current and the next, and that again is not a good state to be in. Think about the worst case scenario, if the venture fails, you have additional skills to build the next venture on, or take up a job. If you lose money—it is really not a big deal because you can always regain it. Money is never gained or lost, it always flows, and fortunes depend on the form in which it is held and for how long. Once it is held for a long time, you get habituated to money and it will flow right back to you. It is like a homing pigeon. No point in going after money, go after the idea, money will automatically follow. But then if you really lost a fortune, it is a great learning experience, because you know how money flows out and the next time you will be even more careful. People who tell me that they made a lot of money, without losing a dime, are people who have either inherited it or have never played with their own money, which is not bad either. Those people were lucky—right time, right place! Or maybe ingenious to make others invest for them to thrive and that is a terrific proposition as well.

Ma Jun[4], director, Institute of Public Health and Environmental Affairs of China, a soft and quiet man, was extremely unhappy with the environmental degradation of Beijing, a city that was ranked 1,035 out of 1,100 international cities in air pollution. In 2006, Ma thought, enough of pushing paper around and decided to do something about it and started a non-profit organization called Institute for Public Health and Environment (IPE). With the help of nine full-time staff, he used the Internet to mobilize China's youth, by creating a network, and an open online source that recorded air, water, and hazardous waste pollution, and he also pulled out 97,000 factories which were in violation of China's green norms. Most of these factories, interestingly, turned out to be sub-contractors for many global multinationals. He tried approaching many of these factoriess to comply, but most of them were reluctant to change, not because of lack of technology, but because there was no mindset to change. So he started approaching the MNCs by sharing the data and requested them to regulate their supply chains and work with the factories to stringently follow environmental guidelines. Thus, Walmart became one of the first global MNCs to tie up with IPE. By 2008, most global multinationals like Levi's, GE, Coca Cola, Microsoft, Nike, and such others tied up with IPE. Local contractors were asked to report environment-related data and made MNCs accountable for best practices in environment management. Ma says that the initial assumption that hazardous metal pollution was from mines or smelters was wrong. The real problem was coming from factories making global IT equipment. For example, factory workers started suffering from nerve damage from a chemical called n-hexane, which was used to clean the touchscreens and they identified 29 major technology brands with hazardous operations and soon enough they learnt that Apple had subcontracted Taiwanese manufacturer, Wintek, to make touchscreens. So Ma wrote letters to CEOs of all the 29 companies and gave them the data of environmental degradation. Many firms started engaging with IPE, but Apple refused any confirmation of relationships with these factoriess owing to supplier confidentiality. Then Ma sent a second letter to Jobs and there was no response. Soon Ma unleashed a social media campaign titled, 'The other side of Apple' along with videos on the Internet, and pretty soon Apple came up with the Supplier Responsibility Progress report and finally confirmed the case of poisoned workers, but didn't respond to environmental pollution. Meanwhile, Tim Cook took over in August 2012, and just before Ma released 'The other side of Apple: Part 2', Apple agreed to work with IPE. A few months later, Ma Jun won the prestigious Goldman Prize for his efforts in improving the environment.

When the force of an idea is just so powerful, the world will buckle to serve the purpose of humanity. The qualities that differentiate people—fearless attitude, passion, single-minded devotion and the fact that they took a leap of faith to achieve what they set out to do.

In 1965, University of Florida developed a drink that replenished the quantities of water, carbohydrates, and electrolytes, which school students lost from their bodies, during sports events. The drink was named 'Gatorade' from the team Florida Gators. Though initially marketed by Stokely Van Camp, in 1983, Quaker Oats Company purchased it and subsequently in 2001, the company was bought over by Pepsi Co. In 2007, the multi-billion dollar brand started to flatten out, and sales dipped by 10 percent. Fast Company, in June 2012, reported an interesting story. 'In mid-June 2008, Sarah Robb O'Hagan left her job as a general manager at Nike and joined as the president of Gatorade. She joined Gatorade at a time when retailers were up in arms asking the company to do something to boost the sales of the sagging Gatorade brand. Gatorade was spending millions of dollars on mass-advertising. Every other TV slot, every super-bowl slot, Gatorade was up there, but the sales were dropping. The first thing Sarah did was to jump into the numbers and they silently conveyed a story. 15 percent of high-school athletes and 7 percent of weekend marathoners, in total 22 percent of consumers were contributing to 46 percent of all Gatorade sales. Sarah thought, why spend so much money advertising for all and sundry, and apply brand pull only towards the athletically focussed.' As she further thought, she was convinced and went ahead with the strategy and pitched it to her boss, Massimo D'Amore, the then CEO of Pepsi. She told D'Amore, 'It's ok if you want to fire me, but this is what we have to do, and we have to start saying no to a lot of stuff that retailers are asking us to do, that Wall Street is asking us to do, and we just have to serve the athlete and act like a sport performance company. And it is going to be a long, hard journey,' and he understood and said,'Okay, we are in.' She quickly started focusing on coaches who were working with children, who were 11 years and older, an age when children stop playing for fun and start competing. She helped revise lesson plans at over 4,000 sponsored summer camps, tournaments, and connected nutrition with performance. For the older crowd, who were knowledgeable, instead of big budget ads, she started supporting training groups organized by local sports stores. Earlier, the company spent 90 percent of its ad budget on TV, she cut that and put 30 percent on digital ads. They came up with Gatorade edge, a system, which could track individual performance and also draw comparisons with other athletes in the country. She thought that even if 100 athletes change the culture of sports, it is going to be a huge influence. She said, 'Why on earth would you spend money on super-bowl ads, when players are drinking our product during the entire game.' Further she was turning Gatorade into a hub of fitness knowledge and opened up Gatorade Sports Science Institute near the company headquarters in Chicago. The idea was to create a global chain of such high-tech centres where people would come and get tested and these were the same centres where even professional players enrolled and along with them, they took the Gatorade brand ahead. By 2011, sales exceeded $3 billion, a 9 percent increase from the previous year.

Daunting is not the right word for somebody to come into Pepsi, a company take a decision to redefine what the company has been doing for years, and then to turn it around.

The strategy she adopted was 'a win from within', which is a combination of defining Gatorade as a sport athletic brand, work with local groups, bring science and technology to fitness and nutrition, and personalize the experience for masses. Often products and brands start off addressing a specific focus segment, then they become successful, then they expand geographically, but within the same segment, and then they become big. At this point, most companies introduce product and brand extensions to meet the needs of other segments. The strategy flies, newer market segments adopt it, and revenues increase. Meanwhile, niche players start eating into the same segments and chip away at market share until they become bigger, generic brand players. Then the sales drop and new strategies have to be applied. Brands which successfully survive the onslaught of market cycles become generic brands. For example, Coca Cola and Pepsi became any occasion products, almost replacing water to quench thirst. Products like Gatorade are associated with fitness and nutrition. Red-Bull[1] is associated with instant energy.

If you are clear about the strategy and have the confidence to execute it, then if it looks contrarian, take a leap of faith, convince your management, and take it forward.

Here is an important secret, which most people don't realize—managements often don't back strategies, as much as they back the person who is running it. But if you get a nod, make sure you stick to the plan and deliver to perfection. Proposing approaches which are non-conventional or non-traditional and those that ask managements to think radically needs courage, and it comes with an inner strength, a strong belief that what you are proposing is going to work. Cultivate it and it will enhance your runway significantly. That is how you end being a transformational leader.

Interestingly, RedBull[1] is the most popular energy drink with 4.6 billion cans sold globally in 2011, which is more than half the population of planet earth, which is roughly 7.5 billion. If brands can personalize and still make it generic across all segments, then those products stand the test of time. Redbull GmbH is an Austrian company and it sponsors extreme sports such as freestyle motor-cross and cliff-diving. In the fall of 2012, Austrian sky-jumper Felix Baumgartner jumped off from the edge of the space, broke the sound barrier with a speed of 833.9 miles per hour, and recorded his own sonic boom, and Redbull broadcasted the stunt on YouTube. As on April 2013, 33 million people viewed the clip and as on that date about 4,00,000 or more people tweeted about the event.

In an interview with him, post his jump, he says that, 'For the first five and half minutes, it is a free fall and one does not know what happens to the human body when it crosses the sound barrier, so I say a prayer and jump.' Then he goes on to add that he is disciplined, works smartly with a team of knowledge players and specialists, and that gives confidence to his mother, though she is still scared. Take a moment and see the video on YouTube, it is fantastic! Upon landing, he told *USA Today*, 'I feel super light right now, like I just lost 20,000 pounds of pressure off my body, I can't tell you what it feels like to feel that much pressure to be perfect in front of the whole world.'

A leap of faith, to do the impossible requires hard work, smart thinking, an understanding of technology, and listening to lot of specialists. But then once you set out to do the impossible, plan it carefully and execute it to perfection. That perfect ten minute jump was the result of a five year, privately funded space supersonic free-fall programme.

Unless people have confidence in their products and services, it is impossible to be fully transparent. McDonald's[3], especially in Canada, was getting a lot of flak about their food, processes, and practices on the social media space from consumers. On the other hand, the company was spending millions of dollars trying to improve the quality of services and its products, besides introducing a healthier product line in the form of the Real Fruit Smoothie. Somehow the message was not getting across to the consumers. Earlier McDonald's introduced QR codes on its packaging to drive consumers online so that they could read the FAQs about its food quality. But it wasn't helping as much and that is when McDonald's chief marketing officer, Canada, invited the DDB (agency) and team and asked them to think big in terms of building a digital programme to address consumer concerns. McCartney and the DDB team brainstormed along with McDonald's marketing team and introduced a digital campaign on YouTube in the spring of 2012 termed as 'Our Food, Your Questions'. About 17,000 questions were posed online and a team of experts from McDonald's answered them in a one-on-one interaction with consumers. The company even posted videos on how chicken nuggets are tested for bones and consumers also could view a 24,000-acre family farm where cows roamed. That seemed like a shift in corporate culture in driving more transparency. Companies have to be extremely careful when they run such arduous and large scale transparency campaigns. Each and every answer has to be truthful, candid, and should reflect reality, because the company has thrown open the gates for consumers to ask, a challenge it should now be willing to subscribe to positively and truthfully. A small mistake could go viral and tarnish the image of the company forever. Unlike the physical arena, in the digital space, memories are longer and can be easily evoked at the click of a button. To undertake and run such programmes and come out unscathed, one needs to develop trust in one's ability to manage difficult questions, uncertain situations and unmanageable and irascible people. You need to have maturity, patience, and the ability to rally people around to come out unscathed. However, if one doesn't take that leap of faith, the journey is never fulfiling.

Unlearning

'Be very, very careful what you put into that head, because you will never, ever get it out.'

—**Thomas Cardinal Wolsey**

HERE IS AN INTERESTING parable from Zen Buddhism. 'The master Nan-in had a learned visitor who came to inquire about Zen. But the visitor kept talking about his own ideas with the knowledge acquired from his past. After a while, Nan-in served tea. He poured tea into his visitor's cup until it was full, then, he kept on pouring. Finally the visitor could not restrain himself. "Don't you see it's full?" he said. "You can't get any more in!" "Just so," replied Nan-in, stopping at last." And like this cup, you are filled with your own ideas. How can you expect me to give you Zen unless you offer me an empty cup?'

Unless you unlearn constantly, your cup will be full of

your own ideas picked up from your past and springing from your own thoughts. How can one fill your cup with any new wisdom? Some ideas and thoughts have to be banished, some refuted for new seeds to sprout and blossom. One day these flowers too will wither and the new shall see sunshine. That is the essence of transforming knowledge into wisdom. Lao Tzu, founder and philosopher of ancient China, author of *Tao Te Ching* and founder of philosophical Taoism said, 'To attain knowledge, add things every day. To attain wisdom, subtract things every day.'

Learning something new is not easy, but letting go of something which you have already learnt, termed as 'unlearning' is even harder. Often people think that what worked in the past may work in the present and the future too. How many times have we not heard the sentence, 'Nothing seems to work here, in our previous company we did this and it worked brilliantly!' Most corporate executives, when they take up new assignments in a new company, are in a hurry to implement what they already did before. They are happy to run a few transactions and get some quick wins.

I read an interesting corporate story sometime back. The outgoing CEO prepared three envelopes to be handed over to the new CEO when he joined, with two caveats viz., each envelope had to be opened in intervals of twelve months and secondly, the envelopes had to be opened only if things didn't go too well. When the new CEO arrived, he was presented the first sealed envelope, which he tore open. It read, 'restructure'. So he went about restructuring the whole business the way he did in his previous company. The results were dismal and within the next one year, he opened the next envelope and it read, 'fire away'. So the CEO got rid of his top management team which he thought was responsible for the dismal results. Things didn't improve and within the next one year he opened the last envelope and it read, 'You haven't unlearned. Make three envelopes for the next.'

Forbes online, in June 2012, carried an article by Erica Dhawan[1]: 'What does it mean to unlearn?' 'Unlearning is not exactly letting go of our knowledge or perceptions, but rather stepping outside our perceptions to stand apart from our worldviews and open up new lenses to interpret and learn about the world.' But since people often build incrementally based on past learning, stepping outside the perceptions to take an unprejudiced fresh look, especially from the cacophony produced from layers and layers of accumulated information is a very difficult proposition.

Starbucks quickly unlearned the thinking of the old way of doing business, which was to serve the best coffee that any consumer wanted. Instead, they quickly moved on to providing the experience and created a place between home and office, where people could hang out, surf the net, converse, relax, and spend time with each other. They soon became 'exhilaration cafes'. If somebody were to ask, 'What business is Starbucks into?' my answer would be that they are in the 'human experience' business, and coffee and related products are the medium. And this could happen because Starbucks moved beyond coffee, it quickly unlearned that a company cannot compete on a product alone. Companies now compete to gain attention at experiential levels.

Wipro Corporation is a global conglomerate and as on April 2013, its revenues stood at $7.88 billion and the market capitalization was nearly $24 billion. The company is a global leader in Information Technology (IT) and is known for some of the best practices in IT delivery and human resource practices. I recently met with Pratik Kumar, their global head of HR, and as we were conversing, he said something profound, 'Wipro, over the years, has retained the core philosophy of doing business, but with changing times, it has been able to unlearn and abandon many practices, systems and methods.' I guess that is Wipro's competitive edge. Not many corporations have the ability to retain the core philosophy and still manage to unlearn rapidly enough to be a global leader. Unlearning is the starting point of abandoning what we don't want, doesn't work, or is not fruitful in the long-run. Technology obsolescence hits every 18 months, companies can end up with myriad and complex systems, which may or may not talk to each other. The right will not know what the left hand is doing. Over a period of time, companies have to keep rationalizing, unlearning, and importantly take planned decisions on what systems and processes need to be abandoned and what to be retained. It takes a lot of effort, money, and resources to simplify complex systems, so unless CEOs and CIOs quickly unlearn and adapt new ways of doing things, it will prove expensive for companies.

More than a decade ago, just when emails were becoming popular as a mode of communication, the secretary of a CEO would print all his emails and keep it on his desk and he would write his responses on the paper. Then she would type them and send responses, which is a colossal waste of time, paper, and energy. Soon enough, with social pressure from senior management, he learnt how to use emails and started sending one-liners. Later he remarked, 'I had to tell myself that paper is past and email is the future.' Unless people adapt to the present and potentially the future, as it unfolds, they will stifle innovation.

If there is one big obstacle to innovation, that is 'unlearning'. The human brain is conditioned to perform real-time analytics and deduce patterns from the past. Often it builds on the existing, and this impedes absolute fresh thinking. Probably an apple had to fall on Sir Isaac

Newton's head for him to exclaim 'gravity!' He probably had to overcome the unquestionable commonly accepted law that, 'All objects fall to the ground', and probably until then nobody asked the question, 'Why?' Unlearning has the capability to disturb the existing and arrive at disruptive new technologies.

In the process of designing products, Steve Jobs, the legendary CEO of Apple, started by asking his team, 'What do we want?',instead of asking 'What can we produce?' Alan Kay, GUI pioneer and former fellow, Apple Advanced Technology group says, 'Steve understands desire.' When it comes to product design, Jobs essentially focussed on fresh breakthroughs by starting from 'desire', which clearly means that the thinking pattern starts from the 'new' and doesn't build on the existing. And 'desire' leads to 'delight'. Starting from the new is a powerful 'unlearning' process, just look at where Apple is today. Between September 2010 and September 2012, Apple US grew from $65.22 billion to $156.50 billion; a 239.95 percent growth. In the last ten years, Apple has been growing at 37.7 percent year-on-year and has even touched one of the highest global market capitalizations of $500 billion. And what was Apple built on? Human desire! And this requires unleashing the phenomenal energy of forward thinking, based on the concept of unlearning of the past.

Let me give you the instance of one of our consulting engagements. We were redesigning new titles, levels, and competence grids for a company which recently went through a merger. Now, our engagement was to advise the company on how to build an equitable grid that would map all the employees to a common system of levels and competencies. Meanwhile, the sponsor, one of the senior vice presidents sent us an entire file containing levels, titles, competence grids, and said, 'We had something similar in one of my earlier companies, and it worked wonders. Let's see if we can implement the same – quick and easy'. However, I was not very convinced because what works for a company, may not work for another. One has to understand the current requirements and accordingly work on bettering the systems. Nevertheless, despite our goading not to pursue the track, the senior vice president was hell bent on implementing it, since he thought it was much quicker to implement something that was already deployed earlier painlessly. He made a slight tweak to the documents in a hurry to wrap up the initiative; a quick win, he thought—he went ahead and presented it for global implementation team. The amount of resistance was mind-boggling with ensuing cat-fights and the cold-wars bruised many egos and the assignment turned cold turkey for a while. I almost thought of dropping it. What is the point in pursuing something that was doomed at take-off? Importantly, nobody likes to implement a system which they have not been consulted on. People like to know where they fit in the overall scheme of things. Many were scared that the proposed system would underpin their existing levels to a lower ticker, and that builds huge insecurity in the environment. A couple of months passed, it was communicated that a fresh look at the initiative would be taken and the CEO called us and asked us to revamp and he said, 'Go slow, go easy, we are not in a rush.' I guess he got the point. This time we started with a survey and sought suggestions of what the senior and middle management thought we should be doing. We then took the drafts and ran it past them again and concluded the competence grids in three rounds of discussion. The final product was not substantially different from what the senior vice president presented, but what people didn't want to hear was, 'It worked in our previous firm, it will work here too.' Maybe, maybe not. The fundamental nature of human beings is to be asked and consulted. On concluding the exercise, the senior vice president walked up to me one day and said, 'What an experience, I guess one has to unlearn the past and start afresh.'

Here is another interesting incident, a newly joined executive vice president (EVP), of a $4 billion MNC, head of a large business unit, on his first day at work, called for a meeting of all his business executives and dramatically scribbled on the white board '$400 million' and circled it. He then threw the chalk out of the window. Everybody started wondering. The new EVP said, 'I threw the chalk because I don't want to make any changes to that number.

And that number is the new target for this financial year!' The head of sales asked, 'May I ask a question?' The EVP smiled and replied, 'I expected the first question from you Steve, ask any question, without changing the number on the board. All I want to hear is how do we achieve it?' The head of sales smiled and asked, 'How did we arrive at that number?' The new EVP cheekily replied, 'It was the same target that we accomplished in my previous company.' Everybody smiled, even Steve did. Nobody said anything and within six months, four senior executives left, including Steve. The EVP termed the attrition as 'restructuring' and the quitters joined competition. 'Tyrant', they remarked in their exit interviews, referring to the EVP. The new EVP recruited people who he said were 'stars' from his previous organization and they started applying the same strategies that they had applied in the past. In the first year, market share dipped by 7 percent and attrition crossed 12 percent globally. The CEO called for a meeting with the HR head and the EVP left within the next two quarters. What works in the past may not work in the future. If executives don't unlearn, companies struggle.

It is important to retain the wisdom garnered in the past and let go of the transactions that led to it. There are a million ways to get to the point of inflection. At the end of the day, learning is not a straight line or even a curve. It is about connecting the available dots in a given ecosystem. Transaction is about 'specificity' and 'wisdom' is the 'fresh whiff of thought', which has not transcended earlier, until an opportunity showed up.

During my childhood, I once watched a magician perform on the stage and I almost caught him in the act and pronounced my prowess. At the nick of time, he quickly spun his wrist, changed his tack, and my conception of the trick fell apart and I was left baffled. I asked, 'How did you do that?' He grinned and said, 'Same trick doesn't get repeated twice. Every time it has to be something new, where is the novelty otherwise? Forget what you learnt already; see if you can catch the next?'

Too much reliance on what you did earlier stifles newer thoughts and not taking anything from the past makes people re-invent the existing, and both will not achieve the desired results.

Let me give you another example. I was using Windows machines for more than a decade and one day, a close friend told me, 'If you want to write effortlessly, pick up an Apple MacBook, the interfaces are fantastic, and the ease of use is world-class.' I went to an Apple Store and the salesman did a great job, I ended up purchasing the MacBook and came home. I used the Mac for couple of days, called the salesguy and grumbled hard and bored him to death. I even asked, 'Can I return the Mac Book? Could you help sell it for a discount to any customer of yours who walks in?' Jake, the salesperson patiently listened to me and said, 'Sir, you will have to forget Windows and start getting used to Mac. I promise you, once you get used to Mac, you will never go back to a Windows machine again.' I thought this was his continuing sales pitch and I kept quiet with a lingering discomfiture in my mind. Like most of us, I also don't read user manuals, because they are a pain, but this time, I started reading the user manuals about system preferences and interfaces and all that. It took me half a day to assimilate what was written and I started experimenting with the Mac. Within the next week, I was proficient in using Mac. Today, when somebody gives me a Windows machine, I find it hard to run through it efficiently. I am not saying either of them is better than the other, but then it takes time to unlearn to adapt to the new.

Kathy Sierra, American programming instructor and game developer, and her partner Bert Bates are cocreators of *Head First Series of Books*. In her blog, she highlights that in the 1970s, it was how well one could learn, in the 1990s and 2000s, it was how fast and how much one could learn. In the future it will be how quickly one can unlearn.

Interestingly, if one analysed the selection criteria at university examinations for job interviews, in the 80s, prominence was given to learning ability. In the next two decades university examinations focused on the quantum of learning and the speed with which problems were analysed, dissected, and solved. It was a combination of volume, assimilation, and speed. However, in the recent years, there has been a shift. So, in addition to learning ability, speed, and quantum of subject understanding, companies are laying emphasis on the ability to unearth problems, which one can creatively solve and also seize newer opportunities, given the context of rapid change in technology and economics in a globally transforming world.

Further, Kathy says that her partner Bert Bates is a very good 'go player'. Bert Bates, a twenty year experienced veteran java developer, coach, and instructor says that 'Those who progress the most in that game are those who are most willing to leave behind the strategies and tactics they've come to rely on at each previous level. It is a constant cycle of learning and unlearning.'

Kathy writes that while she was studying the Parelli Natural Horsemanship Programme, she observed that she was made to start from square one, which included riding while sitting on the horse's back, with nothing but a halter and lead rope and no bridle, allowing the horse to go wherever he wanted. Those first forty hours helped her unlearn the habits most people are taught, which includes pulling on the reins to stop, and importantly, to unlearn the need to be in control.

She was bang on! When people unlearn and place themselves in newer situations, ambiguity increases and people feel a loss of control and insecurity creeps in, that is when the mind reverts to stacking up on the existing. But precisely that is the moment that one needs to catch, make the transition to the new, and let go of the past learning.

Unlearning has another interesting dimension. Jack Uldrich[2], a renowned global futurist, independent scholar, and bestselling author in his blog, 'Unlearning is Uncomfortable' writes that, 'In 2007, amidst sky-rocketing fuel prices and a shaky economy, General Motors realized that a smaller, eco-friendly car, designed for urban females might be worth developing. To better understand these customers, the company put its male designers and engineers in the shoes of their female customers, literally! They were required to dress in drag in order to better understand what females were experiencing as they struggled with heels, dresses, morning coffees, and young children. The famed design firm, IDEO, has been employing this tactic for years but it is an excellent unlearning tactic. In many cases, unlearning requires you to see and experience things from another person's perspective. One way to do this is to literally put yourself in their shoes. Such tactics might be uncomfortable but I'd argue that they are a lot less uncomfortable than losing out to a competitor who was able to design a new successful product because it was able to unlearn.'

Unlearning at times becomes easier when people switch roles and the landscape. The head of delivery and head of operations of a large IT firm were at constant loggerheads with each other. Both were great performers, both had strong views, and both wanted to do their best for the company. Outside of work, they were buddies, but at workplace, they couldn't fathom each other's perspectives. The CEO tried making them work together for a while and when things got overheated, the CEO of the firm asked them to switch roles. With much reluctance, they switched roles and within a few months, they started to see the intricacies of each other's perspective. To that extent, head of delivery, Bryan, said to a close friend, 'I spent the first ninety days just unlearning all I previously thought was the right way to approach.' Now Bryan and Dave are buddies both outside and as well inside the work place. Switch roles, switch places, switch methods, and at times it helps unlearn faster.

CoCubes is India's largest online end-to-end mobile enabled hiring and assessment platform. It connects students with companies and helps companies assess talent. Initially, when the young founders Harpreet and Vibhore started the company, they were of the lofty ideal that educational institutions are meant to create knowledge and institutions should not be charged any professional fee for getting students jobs with reputed firms. They chugged along for two years with this philosophy, but soon realized their folly that they were missing out on precious revenues—they quickly had to unlearn and unshackle themselves from their past idealistic thoughts. They realized that private institutions were in the business of making money by imparting education, so they started to charge the educational institutions and revisited their business model. Even at that time, they did not realize that they could charge the corporates a professional fee for getting students on their roll. Harpreet, cofounder and CEO of CoCubes says, 'After five years of starting the company and having signed 400 plus customers on the corporate end, having built a team of sixty people—educating them about why corporate should not be charged a fee, one fine day we took a U-turn. We went back to the corporates and said that we had to charge them for services, and since then the orporate revenue has grown 250 percent. People who couldn't deal with this change left, and we had to hire folks who believed in the new direction of the firm.'

Intrinsically in any business, there is nothing such as rules of the game. They keep changing and evolving as long as the management has an open mind to unlearn—to discard the past and embrace the change.

Let me end this with Mark Twain, my favourite author 'Two things seemed pretty apparent to me. One was that in order to be a pilot, a man had to learn more than any one man ought to learn; and the other was that he must learn it all over again in a different way every twenty-four hours.'

LISTENING

'A good listener is not only popular everywhere, but after a while he knows something.'

—**Wilson Mizner**

AS ON MARCH 2013, Starbucks operates close to 20,891 outlets in 62 countries and has 1,49,000 employees with total revenues ending fiscal 2012 at close to $13.29 billion. Howard Shultz, the founder, chairman, and CEO of Starbucks coffee, visits thirty to forty Starbucks stores every week and feels that the leader should instill enthusiasm about the vision of the company. He says, 'The time I spend with people is the single most important thing I am doing.' Incidentally, Starbucks extends healthcare benefits to even part-time employees. So what does Howard do when he is with people? Listen! Otherwise how would he ever get to know what his customers feel about Starbucks, or for that matter assess the emotional health of the company?

Marshall Rosenberg in his book *Non-violent Communication* says, 'Studies in labour management negotiations demonstrate that the time required to reach conflict resolution is cut to half when each negotiator agrees, before responding, to repeat what the previous speaker had said.' What does it mean? Both the parties have to 'listen' to each other carefully and understand what the other person wants.

Steven Covey, a renowned author and global consultant, talks about empathetic listening where he emphasizes the need to understand before being understood. According to him, more than grasping the technique of active or reflective listening, the key is to get into another person's frame of reference.

When people say, 'you aren't listening', often it is not that you aren't listening. It is to do with understanding them, caring for them and trying to do something for them. Here is one of the best quotes on listening by Mahatma Gandhi: 'If we have listening ears, God speaks to us in our own language, whatever that language be'.

In the book *Legacy of Love: My Education in the Path of Non-violence*, Arun Gandhi, quoting his grandfather, Mahatma Gandhi says, 'There was a young boy your age who was always angry because nothing seemed to happen the way he wanted. The boy had his own agenda and his own perspective on everything, and because he was unwilling to recognize the value of other perspectives, he lost many of his friends. No one likes someone who is obstinate and prone to tantrums... This went on for years, until the boy reached an age when his simple tantrums would break out into violent actions. One day he got into a very serious fight and accidentally committed murder. In one moment of thoughtless passion, he destroyed his own life by taking the life of someone else. This is what can ultimately happen when people allow themselves to give free rein to anger. Now is the time for you to learn to listen and to cooperate. There will always be another point of view besides our own, sometimes right, sometimes wrong, and we must develop the capacity to pause calmly and evaluate.'

Between April 2007 and April 2010, Medtronic's (pharmaceutical company in the US) revenues grew from $12.2 billion to $15.8 billion, a 30 percent growth with a consistent bottom line. Apparently, William Hawkins III, the CEO spends almost 50 percent of his time dealing with people issues. What does he do most of the time? Listen and attend!

I had the first-hand experience of seeing John Michael Lawrie, chairman and CEO of the $16 billion CSC Corporation, in action, when he took over as the CEO of Misys in 2006–07. For the first thirty days he didn't open his mouth. He met customers, partners, and employees and listened to them. He realized that he was in a deeper mess than what he thought he was in. He engaged McKinsey, BCG, and other experienced consultancies and asked them to dig through the internals and present facts for him, the unedited version—the real truth. He spent endless hours listening to the information that was poured out to him. Fathoming the work involved, when McKinsey presented the work group strategy that evening, at dinner, he remarked, 'Jeez, all the listening is re-emphasizing the journey ahead.' He went and met employees in almost every office across the globe and listened to them. When he came to the Bangalore office, he held small group meetings and ensured that he was listening to one and all. He would briefly explain the strategy he was pursuing, set the context for a management discussion and say, 'Now that you know what is on my mind, tell me what is on yours.' Throughout the discussions, he would listen and diligently make notes.

I believe true leaders have an amazing capability to listen. If you don't cultivate the habit of listening, it would be impossible to be a leader. The 50–30–20 rule is 50 percent of the time you should listen, 30 percent of the time you should ponder, and in the remaining 20 percent time you should speak.

Herb Kelleher[1] was the legendary CEO of South West Airlines, a company that was profitable for thirty consecutive quarters—a feat no other airline in the US has ever achieved. Herb realized that blame-game would compartmentalize the departments and hurt the company, especially when the delay of a plane taking off is attributed to a particular department. So, the company devised a method where the blame was not attributed to any particular department. People had to just tick on the category 'team delay'. That meant almost everybody and every department responsible for getting that particular plane off the ground was held responsible. So people automatically started listening to each other, tried to understand each other's problems and most planes took off on time. When you don't blame, listening and overall efficiency improves.

I personally believe that one of the other biggest obstacles to listening is 'blaming or pointing fingers'. The moment you blame or point fingers, listening goes out of the window. Even evaluation and strong judgement precede the 'blame culture'. Once the mind is corroded with judgement, it becomes impossible to listen, because one has to let go of the preconceived notions and that is very difficult. The cup should be empty for somebody to pour essence into it. What do judges do most of the time? They follow the 50:49:01 method. They listen 50 percent of the time, read for 49 percent of the time, and pronounce judgement during 1 percent of the time.

Bob Nardelli delivered some of the best operational results during his tenure as the CEO of Home Depot. During his tenure, revenues increased from $45 billion in 2000 to $81 billion in 2005, and earnings after tax rose from $2.58 billion to $5.84 billion. But his communication style was critical and autocratic. He downsized employees with experience in trade and replaced them with part-timers with little or no experience, and this didn't cut ice with employees or the public. Finally, in January 2007, the board asked him to leave.

Charlie Weis signed a 10-year contract with Notre Dame's as a football coach. It was a $35 million contract, starting in the 2006 season and ending in 2015. Thanks to his team's successes, in 2005, Weis won the Eddie Robinson Coach of the Year award, selected by Football Writers Association of America. On November 30, 2009, Weis was fired because of poor team performance. What happened? Many attributed it to poor communication and listening skills.

Sometimes listening is about being available to people. During a skip level meeting, members of a project team said, 'Joe, our project manager is insensitive, he is slave driving us.' Later I asked Joe to meet me and informed him what the team felt; obviously I didn't share the names. He told me that unless he followed the gruelling schedule, the project would come under intense flak from the customer and that he didn't have any option but to drive people hard. He further added, 'Even I am struggling, I am in my cabin almost 14 hours a day, working very hard, but I don't complain, right?' I asked, 'Do you spend most of the time in your cabin?' He became slightly defensive; 'Of course I do meet people, if that is what you are implying.' I veered a little bit and suggested, 'Why don't you move out of the cabin and sit with your team?' He gave me lots of reasons as to why he cannot move out of the cabin. But I insisted that he experiment for a few weeks by sitting along with his team members. A few weeks passed and I decided to have lunch with him at his bay. We shared what we brought from home. Seeing us have lunch, a few of the team members gathered and we asked them to join in and slowly the crowd increased and soon almost fifteen people were having lunch with us. I realized that the team was cracking jokes, having fun, and the tension that they expressed earlier didn't seem to surface. To the extent that a team member said, 'Joe is the best manager we have. He is always available, works with us, and helps us.'

Alan G. Lafley[2] served as chairman of the board, president, and CEO of P&G for almost a decade before retiring in 2010. During his stewardship, market capitalization doubled, the number of billion dollar brands grew to 24, and P&G became one of the ten most valuable companies in the world. *Chief Executive* magazine awarded Lafley the CEO of the year award for 2006. He was instrumental in revitalizing P&G by focusing externally on consumers with his slogan, 'Consumer is the boss'. He is a fantastic listener, travelled the globe, listened to his employees, consumers, retailers, and wholesalers, and introduced the culture of innovation as everybody's job.

Listen to the corridor conversations carefully; they reflect the pulse of the company. A close friend told me this story. 'Once while passing along the corridor, I noticed that a few managers were having a blast of a time. I decided to join. After a few minutes they started commenting and having fun at the expense of another senior manager who seemed to be in a relationship with a lady employee. I casually asked, "Is that true?" That put people on the defensive, because I was asking an affirmative question. Most said that it was hearsay. But it got recorded in my mind. But since he was a senior colleague, I mentioned it to him and tried counselling him to keep his extra-curricular activities outside the office. He denied having any relationship. I told him, that it was up to him to figure this out and not get into trouble. But then within a month or so, the lady employee complained of harassment and he left the company.'

Despite all preoccupations, one has to learn to compartmentalize thoughts and learn to listen actively. Here is an interesting incident from when I was working as a strategy consultant for Coopers & Lybrand, a big consulting firm that merged with Pricewaterhouse to become PWC. During one of the intense projects that we executed for Ranbaxy Labs, a $2 billion pharmaceutical company, I was quite preoccupied with making a very large and complex project plan with multiple tracks. Meanwhile, our project head, Hari, called me to join the project status review meeting and I requested him to give me another thirty minutes because I was in the midst of planning and didn't want to lose continuity of thought. But he insisted that I attend the meeting. So, I stopped the project plan mid-way and went for the meeting. During the meeting, I just couldn't concentrate and spent the whole hour conceptualizing the project plan in my mind. I couldn't even hear a single sentence of what was being discussed. I just nodded involuntarily to what was being said, the auto-response all of us are used to. Suddenly all of them turned towards me expecting me to respond, and since I wasn't paying attention, I didn't even know what the question was. I said, 'Excuse me, but could you please repeat the question?' Hari repeated the question, and I struggled with my response. I said, 'I am sorry guys, but I wasn't listening to what was being discussed.' Hari grinned and said, 'I guess your mind is still on the project plan. Go, finish it and meet me.' I left the room and later met with Hari. He said something very interesting, 'TGC, if you have to grow in life, you will have to learn to compartmentalize ideas, work, and time because information has to be absorbed as and when it comes. Unless you learn to compartmentalize, listening would be a problem.' I nodded affirmatively. What he said was completely true.

One day, my 9-year-old came and started talking animatedly about the Indian Premier League (IPL) matches (they are a summer rage anyway!), and I was busy working on my laptop. I didn't want to disappoint him, and so I kept nodding, while I continued to work. Suddenly he stopped mid-way and said, 'You aren't paying attention. I don't want to talk to you.' I looked at him, smiled, and stopped doing what I was doing and listened to what he was saying. Then he continued discussing pitch, batting, bowling, and the entire nine yards. He is a kid, so he was candid enough to say that I wasn't paying attention. Adults don't tell you that, they will be social, but switch off from you. Listening is paying attention to somebody. As simple as that! Some pay attention because they have to. They are being nice and social to you. But in reality, they are not entering the other person's frame of reference. They are waiting for the other person to finish so that they can get on to do what they want to. So paying attention is just not sufficient, *sincerely* paying attention and trying to be empathetic, wins people around. The key word here is 'sincerity'. Often we are so preoccupied with ourselves that we don't listen sincerely. We don't really make the other person feel wanted and important. Besides, we are in a hurry to share so much about ourselves that we end up waiting for the other person to finish so that we can blurt out quickly. I know one senior person who incessantly talks about himself. 'See how well I made this presentation? I impressed the senior management, I was responsible for doing that, I know what to do, let me tell you what to do, you have no idea, let me show you' etc. Most people listen to him out of respect for his position, but given a chance, anyone would love to run away from him.

The biggest obstacle to listening is the ability to overcome the 'I'. Just observe in your work environment, people with a strong 'I' will not let you complete your sentence and jump right in. People have to keep telling them, 'Let me at least finish'. I sometimes wonder how these people reach such senior levels. I guess their other strong skills must have outweighed their listening skills. But according to me their growth would be stunted and they surely would have reached the dead-end. One can go only so far, but not beyond that. Excessive bragging and focus on 'I' is one of the biggest challenges to listening. I coached a senior person who had problems with listening because he was technically far ahead of the curve compared to other team members. While team members were offering suggestions, he would abruptly interrupt and get on to giving directions on next steps. Soon the team members stopped giving any suggestions and looked up to him for direction and next steps. Soon enough, the team members even stopped taking decisions and started pushing all decisions up the hierarchy. It hurt the team and the deliverables started to pile up. In the 360 degree feedback, it was pointed out that he was great technically, but poor in people skills and he felt bad. At times, people with extremely strong technology knowledge, management, and domain skills tend to become poor listeners. I guess the only alternative is to develop patience. Patience precedes listening! Count upto ten before you interrupt, is what I tell people. It helps.

Rendezvous with Simi Garewal was a super hit TV show in India. The format was simple. She interviewed celebrities and they opened up about their private lives on the show. Simple. She asked questions, touched their emotions, and prodded them to speak as she leaned forward to listen intently. She became the viewer and the listener. The celebrity revealed all personal details with the innocence of a child who had been cajoled into spilling his secrets. The audience loved the fact that she managed to get the celebrities to pour out their personal lives in public, and voila, she became an instant hit!

One of my close friends, Dave, works as the head of customer support for a large MNC. To put it crisply, customers love him. I always wondered why he was so popular and decided to observe him a little more closely, and I learnt a few interesting things. Firstly, he is genuinely interested in people. For example, he would diligently note birthdays of clients, friends, and colleagues, and he would be the first to wish them. If you give him a birthday card, he will pin it up on the board and it will be on display for quite a while. You will probably see scores of such cards on his pin-up board. Once, somebody presented him a glass ball with some intricate designs on it and that too landed on his table. His table is full of pictures with family, clients, and friends and all sorts of small memorabilia. Secondly, Dave knows how to smile on the phone and convey that warmth, even when the other person is not able to see him. When on global team conference calls, which are usually long conversations, it is common in the corporate world for most people to turn the phone on mute and do their own thing. At times, I have even heard music, water flushing in the loo, dogs barking, birds chirping, etc., when the mute accidentally came off. When he is on a call, he really participates by diligently taking notes, asks questions, and listens to what is being said intently. At the end of the conference call, he follows up with key stakeholders and summarizes what has been discussed. How many people actually do that? During customer calls, he jots down all the customer issues, repeats to the customer the priorities he is going to work on, and efficiently follows up to completion. So when a customer, in any part of the world, has a problem, she just calls Dave. They have confidence that he will fix their issues. Some issues cannot be fixed and he explains them with valid reasons. Once I asked him, 'How come customers are generally so happy with you?' His answer was very down to earth. He said, 'When a customer is upset, I listen and repeat what they say. I don't refute or argue. Once they are done with what they want to say, I start asking questions and slowly we figure out how to go about solving the problem. Not easy, but patience helps.' Just active and sincere listening could make so much difference.

Once I attended a lecture by Madhavan Nair, chairman of Indian Space Research Organization. The auditorium was packed and he gave a brilliant talk about the future of space programmes. After the talk, he was led to the cafeteria for high tea and snacks. The place was buzzing with people and I observed that Madhavan Nair was quietly sitting in one corner listening to what people were saying. Usually people ask questions as speakers lead the conversation. However, what I noticed was his curiosity to learn. He was firing questions about the research activities being undertaken and he was intently listening and making a mental note of what was being said.

Despite all its research, Amazon[2] forgot to add parental control when it launched Kindle Fire, and within a day, they started getting emails from parents asking for the same. Quickly Amazon got into action and within a month, they added a password that was required to connect to the WiFi. Within the next 90 days, controls for purchase of apps were put in place, and soon controls for viewing were also put in place. Dave Limp, VP at Kindle Amazon, learnt a lesson and then moved on to the next level. He said, 'Let us just not fix the mistake, how do we invent the next level?' Subsequently, when he had an update meeting with Jeff Bezos, FreeTime for kids was conceived. FreeTime essentially is unlimited access to books, magazines, cartoons, comics, and TV time for kids. The whole concept started when Dave listened to how Jeff was trying to discipline his kids on the amount of screen time they were into. Now based on settings, kids can, say watch videos for ten minutes, and read for however long they want to. Most innovations happen because people listen to how other people's lives have developed. Improvisations and what can be done beyond what is available often comes from a keen sense of listening to what the problem or the opportunity at hand is.

The antithesis to listening is 'preaching'. If you get into the habit of preaching, that means you are almost always speaking about yourself, what you did, how successful you were, and what you intend doing. Soon you will be recognized as the world's biggest bore. People have been conditioned to listen to preaching only when they attend the Sunday sermon and that privilege is accorded only to the church. Once they are out of the church, nobody likes to listen to preachers. Most world famous leaders aren't preachers. Do not confuse great oratory or motivational speeches as preaching. Typical motivational speeches are not sermons, but stories of what it takes to get there. Just remember that preaching takes the wind out of the listening skill, because you want to jump right in and tell people what they ought to be doing. The intent is different. Preachers are often perceived as having the 'I know everything' kind of syndrome. At times, mentors and coaches end up preaching. Mentoring and coaching is not preaching. I came across an interesting incident where people started avoiding a senior leader whose mentoring sessions are like preaching sermons. He started telling customers what they ought to be doing and where they were going wrong. Customers heard him for a while and soon after began avoiding him by postponing meetings. He still didn't get it, until management sensitized him to his preachy ways. Preaching is a one-way lane which destroys interaction.

A western Buddhist monk named Ajahn Sumedho[3], talks about 'the sound of silence', an inner sound that emanates within one's mind in the quietness of the self. He calls this the 'primal' sound that rings inside the ears. Deep transcendental meditation helps reach this point where one experiences the sound of the self. When one continually immerses in this state, the mind calms down, distractions reduce, and people are able to see beyond what they usually perceive and hear beyond what is being spoken. That is true listening—listening to the inner voice and the intent behind the expression of every human being.

Innovation

'Innovation is the ability to convert ideas into invoices.'

—**L. Duncan**

MAPPING OF LOCATIONS[1] HAS become the biggest application space that most digital and mobile corporations are vying for. Google has won in the search space, Facebook in the human experience of connecting people, and now the third big fight is who is going to own (digitally) global locales. Nokia's maps cover the most countries with 80,000 data feeds and with 2.4 million uploads a day. In 2008, Google launched 'Ground Truth', a project of massive proportions, which created a property location database of 40 countries using fleets of airplanes, automobiles, and data collected from public and private agencies. The coverage includes 360 degree views, pans, street views, turns, signals, important places, archeological sites, and places of interest. Google wants to map every square millimetre of planet earth. The Apple debacle in the maps space has made Android phones more user-friendly and sought after. Nokia's maps are found in 20 percent of the dashboard navigation systems raking up almost $1.4 billion in sales in 2011. Who ever thought that maps would become such an important facet of online business? That is innovation beyond looking for information, it is innovation related to physical movement.

In 2009, when he was 22, Ben Kaufman found Quirky, an industrial design company based on the idea of crowd sourcing, not just money, but ideas, processes, influencers who built, evaluated, and launched products to local and global market. As on 2013, the community is nearly half a million strong with some 100 inventors. In late 2012, Kaufman raised $68 million from Andreessen Horowitz and Kleiner Perkins and the investments would primarily go into retail experiments to scale crowd sourcing into multi-billion dollar business. The advantages are simple. People propose product designs on the site and community members give feedback on whether the product would fly off the shelves and be successful or simply prove to be duds. It is an online consumer feedback that determines success of a product even before it is launched. Quirky helps design, manufacture, and market these products and sell them online and through retailers. Marc Zech of Germany wanted to wrap up suspended pipes, so he made a design of a rubber band with a hook. Community members liked it, and the product was launched, priced at $9.99 for a cluster of 10. The product has sold quarter million units. Quirky makes money from manufacturing, product designer makes money from the cut and influencing users get a cut for influencing the idea. Stephen Stewart of Belfast designed a simple plastic coral to hold wires from falling behind the desk, which you will almost find impossible to fetch, without moving the table right up. Priced at $9.99 a-piece, it sold 3,50,000 units. Yet another example—Jake Zien of Milwaukee designed a flexible row of rotating sockets to de-congest power outlets. Priced at $29.99, half a million units were sold. Kaufman says that he is capable of introducing two innovative products a week to retailers.

Quirky[2] is a powerhouse of ideas because people come together to create it, validate it, make it, market it, and earn on the fly. That is the power of people coming online to create something innovative. But then nobody thought of integrating people, processes, and products online! Innovation is integration of various forms and may be just one.

Pinterest[2,3,4] is a photo sharing website, where people can upload their pictures related to hobbies, interests, events, food, art, clothing, etc—in short, anything that they would like to share. Ben Silbermann, Paul Sciarra, and Evan Sharp founded the site. In 2009, development of the site began, and it was launched to the first 5,000 users in

March 2010, and within nine months it had 10,000 users. In March 2011, the launch of an iPhone app, about the site did the trick and by August 2011, *Time* magazine listed the site as the 50 best sites of 2011. With 11 million visits per week, in 2011 it became the top ten social network sites driving more referral traffic to retailers than sites like Google. In January 2012, Comscore reported that Pinterest had 11.7 million unique users, which made it the fastest site to break the unique 10 million unique user mark. By March 2012, Pinterest became the third largest social networking site after Facebook and Twitter. Interestingly, in 2012 it was reported that 83 percent of its global users were women. As on February 21, 2013, Bloomberg reported its valuation at $2.5 billion. In comparison, DropBox, a simple storage platform across various devices, was valued at $4 billion in 2011, Twitter at about $10 billion, and room sharing platform Airbnb Inc reportedly had a valuation of about $2.5 billion.

Technology and Internet continue to lead innovation on various fronts and valuations based on unique visitors are skyrocketing. The Internet space continues to be wide open for sites that help people transact, upload, share, save, and experience. At times, simple human experience of uploading pictures of various events becomes such a big business.

Best innovations are the ones that are the simplest. Ending in 2011, Tupperware brands touched revenues of $2.6 billion, and the brand is present in a hundred countries and has a direct global sales force of 2.7 million people. Tupperware is often recognized by the sound of 'burp' when the Tupperware containers are sealed, making it airtight to preserve the food longer. Tupperware is a brand of plastic containers, bowls, and serving dishes used for storage, preparation, and heating of food, mostly for home use. In 1946, Earl Silas Tupper of Leominster, Massachusetts developed the plastic airtight containers to keep food stored longer. The Tupperware containers were made of plastic, rather than the traditional glass and crockery, and it was less likely to break. The 'burping seal' distinguishes the wares from its competitors and is patented by the company. The company tried selling the wares through retailers and marts, but it was not as successful because consumers needed demonstrations to know how the Tupperware 'burp seals' worked. So, in 1948, the company's direct marketing strategy was pioneered by Brownie Wise, former sales representative of Stanley Home Products. She threw outlandish theme parties for women in various neighborhoods to connect and the theme parties provided the perfect backdrop for the sale of Tupperware products. Soon the popularity of these parties exploded and many women after the Second World War, found themselves empowered, connecting and attending the Tupper parties in the post-war business world and were found buying and selling Tupperware products. In the tradition of Tupper parties, in many cities and countries, even today, rallies are held, with the top selling individuals and teams getting recognized and recruited. Almost 75 million people in the world attend these Tupperware parties. The direct sales approach taken by Tupperware was a pioneering approach and it is estimated that the market for selling directly is nearly $50 billion in the US alone and almost $150 billion worldwide. Until then, not many companies were able to come out with an effective direct selling model. This was a model, where mothers and other women working from home, who were part of a neighborhood, became the sales people. Buying the wares was an outcome of Tupper parties that the women in each neighborhood threw for having social connectivity and for feeling a sense of empowerment through doing business. By 1951, the parties, the direct sales, and the demonstration system was working so well that the products were taken off the shelves of retailers and marts and were distributed directly. Quoting from Tupperware website about building a brand, 'The direct demonstration was a welcome diversion for women, whose involvement in the community mostly revolved around their family.' When the cities expanded and suburbs came by, consumers started having backyard barbeques which became a favourite way to pass time for neighbours and get-togethers. By the 60s and 70s more and more women started working in the offices and Tupperware introduced carry cases, office boxes, and plastic carry containers. Basically, the brand moved from the kitchen to the office. In addition, for toddlers and children, Tupperware introduced toys, and for the senior citizens, the instant seal type containers which made it easy for them to open and close boxes comfortably. The Tupperware strategy was to introduce products for women, children, and senior citizens and it kept innovating and filling homes with its products.

Soon microwaves became a household product and Tupperware quickly introduced re-heat containers. Then microwave cooking dishes and modular containers started filling the kitchens. The Tupperware stack cooker was designed to make a three-course meal for four within 30 minutes, using a microwave. Saving time became the core theme of Tupperware, to address the needs of dual working families. In 1990s, when home cooked food came back into focus, Tupperware launched kitchen tools to peel, blend, and cook in a much more sophisticated way. Tupperware even conducted cooking classes, speed classes, value for money shopping, custom kitchen planning, and other such courses at home and for the neighbourhood communities. In 2000s, with rapid urbanization and the advent of the age of technology, Tupperware products can now be ordered from the Internet, can be purchased from retailers and also from large marts. But the direct sales model continues to be the backbone marketing strategy for sales of its products, besides obviously an innovative product line. The company clearly changes with times and that is the mark of an evolving and innovative company.

Tupperware is one of the most innovative companies in the world, which targeted women, home appliances, and direct marketing model, where consumers became both the buyers and the sellers. Essentially with changing times, the company came up with innovative products and never stagnated on the product line. Innovation is about evolving with times, knowing very well what the consumer wants. Importantly, innovation is about staying close to the customer, talking to them constantly, and trying to make products which they want and those that they will buy even before they are made. The new paradigm of innovation is that buyers and sellers are the same people within the same community, buying and selling from each other.

In 2003, three students, Niklas Hed, Jarno Väkeväinen, and Kim Dikert from Aalto University School of Science, Helsinki, Finland, participated in a mobile game development competition sponsored by HP and Nokia. They made a real-time multi-player game called 'King of the Cabbage World' and won. Soon, the trio decided to start a company and work on developing games. Subsequently, they sold the game 'King of the Cabbage World' to Sumea studios. In the same year, the trio decided to start a gaming company and named it Relude. In 2005, they received angel funding and changed the name to Rovio Mobile. In December 2009, the company released Angry Birds, an online game on iPhone, in which the player uses a string shot and releases a bird to break puzzles. Since then, the game has been downloaded 1.7 billion times across platforms and paid downloads were more than 25 percent of overall downloads, making it one of the most sold games on the Internet. The success of the game led to many investors flocking to their door and in March 2011, Rovio Mobile raised $42 million in venture capital funding from Accel Partners, Atomico and Felicis Ventures, and changed the company's name to Rovio Entertainment Ltd. Within a year, it acquired Futuremark Games Studio, and now the company plans to make digital movies of the game. The company also launched product extensions such as Angry Birds Seasons, Angry Birds Rio, Angry Birds Space, Angry Birds Star Wars, etc. Besides the game's popularity was so high that it was used as an advertisement on Microsoft Bing and as a cartoon in the Israeli–Palestinian conflict. Rovio sponsored Formula 1 driver Heikki Kovalainen to unveil the Angry Birds crash helmet in the 2012 season. Hockeybird was the official mascot for the 2012 IIHF ice hockey world championship. Ending 2012, the company clocked nearly $200 million in revenues with nearly $75 million as net income.

My son was completely addicted to the game and so was I for a while. The game became a reason for our family to come together, to laugh, and to share some quality time with each other. It is indeed an incredible innovation of how a game can connect people, make them addictive, and become such a powerful brand in such a short while. Innovation in the connected world doesn't have boundaries. You never know what will strike the chord and how your innovation can be adapted. I expected something like Angry Birds to come from Disney but surprisingly, it came from unexpected quarters. Once successful, I think, companies find it very difficult to change a certain line of thought and try to build incrementally on it. This stifles innovation and impedes people from thinking differently. Unless companies rethink their business strategy in terms of a complete overhaul at periodic intervals, they tend to get stale. Peter Drucker says, 'Embracing the new requires abandoning the past.'

Thomas Cook[5] was born at Melbourne, Derbyshire. He started work very early in life, at the age of ten. He began working at that tender age as a gardener's help, and as a printer at Loughborough. By 20 he became a Bible reader for the county of Rutland. One day in 1836, he decided to stop drinking and became a teetotaler and actively associated himself with the temperance movement. In 1840, he published the Children Temperance magazine, a first of its kind in England. In connection with the Temperance movement, in June 1841, a large meeting was planned at Loughborough. It was then that Thomas Cook had an idea and approached the Midland Counties Railway Company to run a special train from Leicester to Loughborough. The railway company agreed and on July 5,570 passengers paid one shilling per person for a two-way trip from Leicester to Loughborough, and of this payment Cook got a cut for his services. This was one of the first publicly advertised excursions of that kind. With the event creating a stir, many people started to approach young Cook to arrange for excursion trips. Soon, he left the wood business, while continuing the printing business, and for many summers, he organized travels for various parties across the country. Cook thought he should do something on a bigger scale and in 1845, he launched a pleasure trip from Leicester to Liverpool and back, and with opportunities to visit Isle of Man, Dublin, and the Welsh coast. As a part of this trip, he prepared a handbook for all the travellers. While the trip was successful, it had financial implications on the business that Cook had to overcome. Undeterred by the earlier experience of organizing in large scale, he went and organized an even bigger trip for 1,65,000 visitors to visit the Great Exhibition of 1851. Soon he started travels for people across Europe. He opened trips to Switzerland in 1863 and Italy in 1864. Until this time, he was personally conducting all the excursions, but then looking at the size of the business that was growing and the opportunity that it unfolded, he became an agent for selling tickets for England and Europe for people to travel by themselves. By 1865, nearly the whole of Europe was included in the scheme and in 1866, he extended his business to US. For the Paris exhibition, he leased a hotel there and soon began the system of issuing hotel coupons that provided fixed rates for accommodation. In 1872, the company Thomas Cook & Son was formed. In 1891, Thomas Cook died. He had been afflicted with blindness in his declining years. Today Thomas Cook is a nearly $20 billion dollar company, with about 25 million customers globally, 35,000 employees, and a fleet of 93 aircrafts.

Thomas Cook built a market from scratch—the travel and tourism industry. Innovation is seizing an opportunity and building incrementally on it to achieve success. Innovative ideas happen in a flash and then it takes years of innovative best practices to grow, to maintain customers, and to be a world leader. When people start an enterprise, they hardly know where it leads to and many die even before they can see the far reaching impact of what they started off with. The whole idea is to start thinking and thinking fast enough to make the best of any given situation.

Ekso Bionics[7,8] design and manufacture intelligently powered bionic devices, more like robot suits that are strapped on to human bodies to improve the mobility and strength of paraplegics and soldiers. The company was founded by Homayoon Kazerooni, Russ Angold, and Nathan Harding—members of the Berkeley Robotics and Human Engineering Laboratory at the University of California. In the year 2012, they got approval for using these suits in US hospitals and with the CE approval from European Union, the company has also started selling them to rehabilitation centres in the US and Europe. *Wired* magazine selected Ekso as the second most significant gadget of the year in 2010, and in the same year, *Time* magazine included the suit in the 50 best innovations of the year. *Inc.* magazine said that Ekso Bionics was creating the '5 Big Ideas for the Next 15 Years'. Right from its inception, the company has forged partnerships with UC Berkeley and the Department of Defense has given them grants to work on the technology. Ekso Bionics is the pioneer in the field of exoskeletons and has designed one of the most innovative solutions for people to improve their mobility and capability.

Innovation often lifts humanity from the depth of physical, mental, and emotional deprivation. Ekso Bionics is a ray of hope to millions of paraplegics out there for whom mobility is unthinkable. People who come out with ideas for the betterment of humanity always succeed because it puts smiles back on people's faces.

In January 2013, Amy Ryles posted an interesting article on eatbigfish.com. Nicholas Negroponte[6] is founder and emeritus chairman of MIT, Media Labs and also known as the founder of the One Laptop Per Child Association. Negroponte asked the US politicians, 'What, in your opinion, is our most precious resource?' While many answers cropped up, the response kind of converged to one answer and it was 'children', because they, as much as this generation, hold the key to solving world's most challenging problems. However, globally, and more so in Africa, close to 100 million children never make it to first grade. So he came up with the concept of giving free laptops to children around the world—One Laptop Per Child. It was well-received as a form of exploratory education, especially in countries where structured education didn't stack up. But then, like every other programme which gets conceived has to bear a certain criticism, this too had the critics asking: Is this a programme to replace teachers? He never thought about that earlier, but now having been posed that question, he thought, 'Could it really replace teachers?' So he went to Wonchi, Ethiopia with these tablets, which had hundreds of pre-installed applications and distributed them to the children. The children were taught how to switch on the device and how to charge it, and nothing else. Negroponte thought that they would probably end up playing with the boxes the tablets came in. But to his astonishment, within a week, most children were using 47 applications every day and within two weeks, the children were singing ABC songs and guess what, within five months they hacked the Android operating system to enable the camera, which was disabled. Negroponte said, 'You would not have been able to hack the system, nor would I, but they had.'

Power of exploration, to innovate, cannot be underestimated, especially when children are at it. Every generation gets more comfortable with tools and technology compared to the earlier generation. Recently, I went to my friend's place and her 2-year-old, eats her lunch, only if she is allowed to swipe her index finger and play her favourite songs on the iPad. Later, she was standing in front of the television and was swiping her index finger on the TV assuming that every screen can be used in a similar manner. Children have an intuitive understanding of technology and the latest gadgets because they start on a fresh slate, there's nothing to unlearn.

Ben Serotta[9] was 14 when he started building bikes

from his family hardware store. Later he studied frame building at the renowned Whitcomb Lightweights and then moved to Saratoga Springs, NY to make hand-made, custom-built bicycles. Ben is an avid cyclist and inventor himself. His focus was to improve the cycling experience and drive better performance for the rider. Serotta figured out that the perfect bike for every person has to be personalized because the way each person rides a cycle is unique. This concept drove him to create hand-crafted bicycles for each and every customer. So when a customer wants to buy a bike, he goes over to the factory, where he takes a test ride. The movements of the body, the muscle stretch, the tone, the angle, and almost every smallest movement is recorded by a computer, and accordingly a cycle is designed and then on approval, it is hand-made for the customer and hence there is a waiting time when you order for a bicycle at Serotta. This spurred development of oval tubing, customized carbon and titanium frames, and many other such innovations that have changed the face of the bicycle industry and Serotte builds one of the best bicycles in the world. Ben says, 'Since we build bikes one at a time for specific people, we do not have a manufacturing process per se. Instead, we are committed to building a bike for you, a bike that fits you, and performs how you want it to. We begin with no preconceptions, no template. There are no shortcuts or magic formulas. No matter how technologically advanced and race-ready a bicycle is, unless it fits you like a glove, peak performance of the bike and rider will never be realized. Our bikes are 100 percent hand-crafted and we are fanatical about quality control.' Serotta also built bikes for the 1984 Los Angeles Olympic games and subsequently for the Tour de France bicycle events. In 1988, Ben founded the Serotta International Cycling Institute, which trains riders, coaches, retailers, clinicians, and physiotherapists, and the courses incorporate content relating to rider's goals, fitness programmes, physical concerns, body injuries, and sustenance.

Ben has combined a few things to run a successful company viz., passion for bicycles, understanding the engineering behind it, the research that goes into it, personalization, a national brand, and institutionalizing the knowledge garnered. Importantly, he has built a community of like-minded cycling enthusiasts.

Innovation at times unfolds, many times unravels, sometimes is pursued, often stumbled upon, and in Ben's case, it was to have a vision to carry through many facets of execution.

Happiness

'People are just as happy as they make up their minds to be.'

—**Abraham Lincoln**

THE US DECLARATION OF Independence of 1776 says, 'Pursuit of happiness is an unalienable right,' and Benjamin Franklin rightly stated, 'The Constitution only guarantees the American people the right to pursue happiness. You have to catch it yourself.'

Eric L. Zielinski[2], a peer reviewer and published researcher writes in NaturalNews.com—'Research has suggested that 50 percent of our happiness levels are determined by a genetic set point, 40 percent by our intentioned actions, and only 10 percent by life's circumstances (e.g. income, social status, place of residence, age). Taking into effect the science of epigenetics and our ability to turn on and off certain genes, it appears that the 50 percent subject to genetics can be 'altered' or modified by our thoughts and actions. Thus, it remains to be seen that up to 90 percent, our ability to be happy is completely contingent on us.' It is clear that to be happy, individual disposition plays a major role. I guess, despite all circumstances, it is important for people to choose to be happy and discard negative thoughts and behaviours.

Dr Ed Diener, of the University of Illinois, an authority on the research of happiness and well-being, has studied 155 countries and has interesting results to offer. Denmark is ranked as the happiest place on earth. One of the staunch reasons for the high ranking is that the Danes trust each other. During a Gallup world poll, when asked, 'If I lost my wallet, would a stranger return it?' A vast majority of the Danes said, 'Yes!' Costa Rica and some Latin American countries are considered relatively happier. Large extended families and numerous festivals probably make life happier. Though India has some of the maximum number of holidays, festivals, and celebrations in the world, besides a joint-family structure and culturally strong, people-driven supportive social structures, it still ranks 125th on the happiness index, just three notches above Palestine, which for decades has been in a state of constant struggle with Israel. Probably poverty, illiteracy, lack of basic infrastructure, and governance may be upsetting the happiness index for India. According to Gallup polls from 2005 to 2011, these were the happiest countries:[4]

1. Denmark
2. Finland
3. Norway
4. Netherlands
5. Canada
6. Switzerland
7. Sweden
8. New Zealand
9. Australia
10. Ireland
11. United States of America

Research indicates that people live 28 years longer in the happiest nations. Zielinski says, 'These are generally places where people have their own internal standards and are satisfied in their work; using their skills, mastering a career, and loving what they do. Generally, these are not places where there is social competition or excessive materialism, regardless of affluence.' Strong social relationships that people have, seems to be one common denominator across most of these countries. Others include—shorter commutes, green spaces, doing things people love to do, loving and trusting other people, using their skills effectively and productively, a learning environment, and such others.

Dr Edward Diener, also called Dr Happiness, is an American psychologist, professor, author, and works as a senior scientist for Gallup. He says, 'Raising children does not contribute to happiness or sadness. Research shows that if someone desires to have children, then child-rearing will bring great happiness. Whereas, if someone does not like children and the responsibilities associated with raising them, then child-rearing will contribute to sadness.'

So there goes the general norm that raising children is the most pleasurable thing. Dr Myers in his research paper, 'Close relationships and quality of life', published in 1999, says, that it is a difficult experience for parents to raise children especially when they are toddlers and when they grow up and are in their teens. Post these years, once children grow up and leave for higher education and other pursuits, parents experience a sense of relief and have more time for themselves to pursue activities that lead to individual happiness, which could not have been pursued earlier. Referring to the research paper published in 1994 by Hazan and Shaver, he also points that people resist breaking social bonds. Familiarity breeds the like-minded, not contempt. 'Thrown together at school, at summer camp, or on a cross-country bus tour, people resist the group's dissolution. Hoping to maintain relationships, they exchange email addresses, phone numbers, and promise to keep in touch. Parting creates a feeling of distress. At the end of vacations, people hug their waiters or cry when saying goodbye at railway stations.

Social connectivity gives a sense of security, joy, and a fulfilment. To an extent, Facebook has been highly successful because it is connecting people across different places and is making them relive the happy experiences. Aristotle said, 'Happiness is the meaning and the purpose of life, the whole aim and end of human existence.' In the quest for happiness, we try to be socially inclusive by forming the right impressions on people and that develops into strong relationships, which give us security, a sense of belongingness, and the interactions lead us to a state of wellbeing.

Again, it is the same close relationships that give us pain. Peter Warr and Roy Payne in their 1982 research paper 'Experiences of strain and pleasure among British adults', published in *Social Science and Medicine*, asked a sample of British adults, 'What emotionally strained them the day before?' The most frequent answer of negative correlation was 'family'. In the same survey, the positive response by a wide margin was again 'family'. The same family relationships give us heartaches and the sense of greatest joy.

Matt Killingsworth[6,7], while completing his degree at Harvard University, was fascinated to know what makes people happy. He says, 'I began to question my assumptions about what defined success for an individual, an organization, or a society.' He stated that the most reliable method for investigating real world emotions is experience sampling. So, he quickly came up with an iPhone App: www.trackyourhappiness.org. It collects data about the everyday experiences relating to happiness. Prior to answering the questions, users are asked to give some demographic details like age, income, education, marital status, and interesting questions like when they woke up, what time they went to sleep, how many times they liked to be pinged by the App, and how long they wished to continue on the programme of answering these questions. Killingsworth and Gilbert report, 'Then they devised a computer algorithm, which divided each participant's day into a number of intervals equal to the number of samples to be requested, and a random time was chosen within each interval. New random times were generated each day, and the times were independently randomized for each participant. At each of these times, participants received a notification on their iPhone, asking them to respond to a variety of questions about their feelings, thoughts, behaviour, and environment.' Samples were collected on all days of the week and respondents had to answer three questions, of which the first two were posed for all surveys and the third one which was about mind-wandering was posed on a randomly selected subset of samples.

The three questions were:

1. How are you feeling right now? (Rate on a scale from very bad to very good).
2. What are you doing right now? For this question about 22 choices are provided such as—at home, at work, shopping, preparing food, taking care of children, watching TV, and such others.
3. Are you thinking about something other than what you're currently doing? The choices provided were—no, yes, something unpleasant, something pleasant, and something neutral. This question was not posed for all samples, but from time to time on selected sample sets on a random basis.

15,000 people from 80 countries and 86 occupational categories participated in the project and over 6,50,000 real-time reports were collected. On analysis, what Killingsworth and his research team found was that for the average individual, the mind wanders 47 percent of the time, which in turn shortly thereafter produces unhappiness. Basically, 'a wandering mind is an unhappy mind,' he observes.

According to Buddha, the secret to happiness lies in concentrating and controlling one's mind to here and now, and not letting it dwell into the past or dream of the future. Killingsworth's findings may explain why some of the greatest spiritual leaders have always advocated that the foundation of happiness lies in meditation. Meditation helps people stay in the present. Controlled breathing and feeling one's body are two good methods to be in the present.

There are two studies and both have different points of view. Dr Myers' study indicates that married people are obviously much happier than those never married, separated, or divorced. The study also shows that marriage offers the security and comfort of people living together to achieve a common, shared understanding and joy. However, the recent treadmill theory says that people adapt to situations and tend to be happy and express life satisfaction despite any of the above circumstances.

Prof. Daniel Kahneman[14] of Princeton, the world renowned psychologist who won the Nobel Prize in 2002 for his work on psychological impact on economics, wrote a paper titled, 'The sad tale of the aspiration treadmill'. He correlates the relationship between life satisfaction and hedonic pleasures. Dr Kahneman discovered that there is relatively no difference in life satisfaction for most people—'the rich were only slightly more satisfied with their lives than the poor, the married were slightly happier than the unmarried, and neither age nor moderately poor health diminished life satisfaction.' People adapt to the situation they are in and that is the concept of the hedonic treadmill[15,16]. On a treadmill, people march along but don't arrive anywhere. That is the theory of the hedonic treadmill. Regardless of positive or negative life changes, such as taking a vacation, winning a lottery, getting married, having a child, or becoming a paraplegic, the human existence is a constant state of desire, an insatiable quest for the ultimate fulfillment. For those, whose desires are fulfilled, the next journey starts and for those whose desires are not fulfilled, they continue on the same journey. But both feel the same amount of life satisfaction and happiness as they adapt to their situations. The Easterlin Paradox corroborates with treadmill theory. Research shows that the average life satisfaction, over the years is not significantly different between the developed and the developing countries.

Dr Kahneman conjectured that life satisfaction could be better assessed through experienced happiness and that people will always want more no matter how much they already possess. To test the 'adaptation treadmill' theory, Dr Kahneman hypothesized that people with higher standards of living and higher expectations may not have more satisfaction, but could have experienced more happiness. To test this hypothesis, they questioned teachers from a variety of schools from the top-end to the low rank to establish that teachers at top-rated schools experienced more happiness. It turned out that there was absolutely no difference. Results showed that teachers across the paradigm experienced the same happiness but differed in job satisfaction levels. All this boils down to only one thing—experiencing happiness is personality driven and is up to individual disposition.

Dan Ariely, behavioural finance expert and author of *The Upside of Irrationality*, suggests that people should apply the hedonic treadmill theory by investing in long-term memories rather than on materialism. 'If you're deciding between a sofa and a vacation, go for the vacation. You'll quickly get used to the sofa, but the vacation will bring long lasting memories.' Prof. David Myers[10], in his bestselling book, *The Pursuit of Happiness*, wrote, 'The point cannot be overstated: Every desirable experience—passionate love, a spiritual high, the pleasure of a new possession, the exhilaration of success, is all transitory.'

Yale emeritus professor Robert E. Lane says that money cannot buy happiness, and that there is no correlation between income level and happiness at work place. No matter how much people make, they will always want more. The *Forbes* January 2013 issue article, 'Mom Was Wrong: Money Does Buy Happiness. There's Research To Prove It' says—'The Economists, Daniel W. Sacks, Betsey

Stevenson, and Justin Wolfers, found that the relationship between income and happiness is logarithmic. Doubling one's income from $1,00,000 to $2,00,000 increases one's satisfaction by the same amount as doubling his income from $2,00,000 to $4,00,000. Satisfaction would increase if your salary went from $4,00,000 to $6,00,000, but not as much. To achieve the same growth in satisfaction, you'd need for your salary to double again. So, that trader and floor man can both be happy, as long as they both see their wages grow.' But then people struggle way too much to gain that sense of incremental or transitory happiness. So one has to make a choice to go after something and lose sleep for the rest of their lives for that one moment of exhilaration or have a series of exhilarations by having smaller moments of shared happiness.

Dr Myers quotes Bert's research paper, 'Strangers, friends and happiness'. GSS Technical report, Chicago: The National Opinion Research Center, University of Chicago, 1986'. The question posed was, 'Looking at the last six months, who are the people with whom you discussed matters important to you?' Those who named five or more such friends were 60 percent more likely to feel 'very happy' compared to those who shared lesser. Other interesting aspects of relationships and well-being are:

- Happiest university students are those who feel satisfied with their love life.

- Those who enjoy close relationships, cope better with stress, including bereavement, rape, job loss, and illness.
- People report greater well-being if their friends and family support their goals by frequently expressing interest and offering help and encouragement.

Dr John Grohol[12] is the CEO and founder of Psych Central and he shares interesting research findings from his happiness research.

- Money doesn't buy happiness. Once we achieve a certain level of income, which allows us to pay bills and live a lifestyle we are used to, more money doesn't result in more happiness. Two exceptions though – unless the money you acquired significantly places you in a different league with respect to your social rank. Secondly, people who donate money appear to sustain greater levels of happiness, over those who don't.
- People who win lotteries are happy only for short-term and the happiness fades fairly quickly and then people return to their prior level of happiness.
- Research has shown that strong social connections with others are important for our own happiness.
- People who spend their time and money taking a vacation outside home or going on an all-day outing to the local zoo and such others, report higher levels of

happiness than those who buy a bigger house, a more expensive car, or more stuff.

Morgan Frank and his team at the University of Vermont, in 2011, analysed 37 million tweets from 1,80,000 individuals by mapping locations of each individual between homes and work and vacation they took outside. The research result was fantastic—'People tend to be happier when they are further away from home and work.' *MIT Technology Review* states, 'Expressed happiness increases logarithmically with distance from an individual's average location.' Frank and team used a 'scale of happiness associated with common words'. They found that, people who were further away from home or work used more positive words, such as 'beach', 'great', and 'restaurant' and many of these tweets were less likely to contain negative words such as 'no', 'don't', and 'hate'. The team agrees that tweets do not represent actual happiness. However, Frank says that the study 'gives sociologists an unprecedented new window into the human psyche.'

In November 2009, Amazon acquired Zappos[18] for nearly $1.2 billion. Zappos is a very interesting company in aligning company culture with delivering happiness. Tony Hsieh, CEO of Zappos says, 'If we get the culture right, then everything else, including the customer service, will fall into place.' He went ahead and approved the publication of a 'Culture book', where employees described the company's culture, and a copy of the book was distributed amongst all the employees. People in the company enjoy free lunches, a nap room, and free health care. There are spontaneous office parades and managers are expected to spend about 15 percent of their working hours 'goofing off' with employees outside the office. Jenn Lim is the CEO and chief happiness officer of Delivering Happiness, a company co-created with Tony Hsieh to inspire happiness in work and in everyday life. Jenn also worked as a consultant with Zappos and helped create the culture book, besides managing the launch of Hsieh's book, 'Delivering Happiness', a New York Times bestseller, which sold upwards of a quarter million copies and has been published in fourteen languages. Interestingly, Zappos offers $4,000 for anyone to quit after the five-week on-board training programme. Jenn says, 'The thought really makes people think—'Is this the right role for me? Is this the right culture for me? Are these the core values I'm actually going to live by?' Apparently, those who feel that they do not fit in take the money and leave and the method seems to have worked well in weeding out people who did not fit in with the culture. Also, the company doesn't have a script for its employees to respond to callers and encourages spontaneity in interaction. I once called and felt that the lady who was talking seemed happy and had a free-flowing discussion on books and culture, which had nothing to do with the products and services they offered. It left a mark on my mind, that here is a company, which really focuses on culture and happiness of its employees.

Elizabeth Anne Scott[11], a wellness coach, author, and health educator, gives a few tips on enhancing happiness in About.com:

- Most people are happier over weekends. People should pursue what they think they should be doing.
- Positive affirmations work, but not as a rationale for doing something, which you are really not into.
- Happiness is getting what you want, but wants will never stop, having a balance is important.
- Feeling in control won't make you any happier than feeling out of it. So best is to learn to influence people.
- Sleep is good for happiness. Ideally one should have at least 6–8 hours of sleep depending on individual needs. Apparently grateful people have better sleep at night.
- People have the power to talk themselves out of stress, because there are always choices.
- The old adage, 'Laughter is the best medicine' works.
- Positive emotions lead to a more satisfying life.

As we can see, there is a plethora of research out there, and for people who are in pursuit of happiness, four things will help[13,14,15]:

- Choose to be happy. It is a choice that you can make irrespective of any circumstance. A lifetime is consumed in unhappy pursuits, as the choice to keep happy slips us by.
- Develop strong bonds with family, friends, and coworkers—which includes building trust, being grateful, spending time with them, laughing, and enjoying the journey.
- Enjoy the present and not the past and the future. Do this by focusing on challenging work, which you are passionate about—perhaps a goal to accomplish, an innovation to work upon, a delight of a human experience, which you can light.
- Chase the experience of life rather than that big house or that sexy looking car which has diminishing happiness value. Pursue activities that add up to well being—watch movies, listen to music, cultivate a hobby, go on a drive, take a vacation, build Lego, paint, write, compose, pursue photography, go bicycling, and such others.

At a very philosophical level, true happiness is attaining 'Nirvana', what the Zen masters strived for thousands of years. Buddha said, 'I consider the positions of kings and rulers as that of dust motes. I observe treasures of gold and gems as so many bricks and pebbles. I look upon the finest silken robes as tattered rags. I see myriad worlds of the universe as small seeds of fruit, and the greatest lake in India as a drop of oil on my foot. I perceive the teachings of the world to be the illusion of magicians. I discern the highest conception of emancipation as a golden brocade in a dream, and view the holy path of the illuminated ones as flowers appearing in one's eyes. I see meditation as a pillar of a mountain, Nirvana as a nightmare of daytime. I look upon the judgment of right and wrong as the serpentine dance of a dragon, and the rise and fall of beliefs as but traces left by the four seasons.'

ADVOCACY

'Never be afraid to raise your voice for honesty and truth and compassion against injustice and lying and greed. If people all over the world...would do this, it would change the earth'.

—**William Faulkner**

IN THE 19TH CENTURY, it was about overpowering and revolution. In the 20th century, it was obstinacy, strikes, and non-cooperation. In the 21st century, it is advocacy and influencing. Unless people advocate for a cause and involve a large community to participate, the community isn't going to change and the country never will. Advocacy needs leadership of thought and influence. Advocacy also needs a strong ability to network, reach out to people in power, and influence them to make a change. Advocacy also needs money, but that is the least of the problems.

For proper causes such as alleviation of human suffering, creation of wealth, and getting equitable justice—money flows.

Mark Zuckerberg[1], founder and chief executive of Facebook, is also the founder of fwd.com, an initiative pushing for immigration reform in the US to give greater opportunities to world citizens with strong talent and intellectual potential to transform America in the new millennium by leveraging on knowledge capital. On April 11, 2013, Zuckerberg wrote in *Washington Post* that he was teaching a class on entrepreneurship at an after school programme in his community, where middle-school students put together business plans, made their products, and even got an opportunity to sell them. One day he asked, what they thought of going to college. One of the students said that he may not be able to, because he is undocumented. Apparently, his family was from Mexico and they moved to the US when he was a baby and they didn't have papers. This was the case with many in his community.

Mark says, 'These students are smart and hardworking, and they should be part of our future. This is, after all, the American story. My great grandparents came through Ellis Island. My grandfathers were a mailman and a police officer. My parents are doctors. I started a company. None of this could have happened without a welcoming immigration policy, a great education system, and the world's leading scientific community that created the Internet. Today's students should have the same opportunities—but our current system blocks them. In a knowledge economy, the most important resources are the talented people we educate and attract to our country. To lead the world in this new economy, we need the most talented and hard working people. Given all this, why do we kick out more than 40 percent of math and science graduate students who are not US citizens after educating them? Why do we offer so few H-1B visas for talented specialists that the supply runs out within days of becoming available each year, even though we know each of these jobs will create two or three more American jobs in return? Why don't we let entrepreneurs move here when they have what it takes to start companies that will create even more jobs?'

So, Mark along with a bunch of Silicon Valley veterans—Reid Hoffman, Eric Schmidt, Marissa Mayer, Drew Houston, Ron Conway, Chamath Palihapitiya, Joe Green, Jim Breyer, Matt Cohler, John Doerr, Paul Graham, Mary Meeker, Max Levchin, Aditya Agarwal, and Ruchi Sanghvi—started fwd.us, and this group raised $25 million, advocating for this cause. In this case, the idea was to attract the best of world talent to the US so that it benefits the nation, specifically the Silicon Valley eco-system. What do business people do when the systems are preventing them from getting talent or creating news businesses—start an advocacy group and influence the government.

GBC Health[5,6] is a coalition of more than 200 member companies and organizations committed to investing their resources to making a healthier world, for employees, for communities they work, and for the world at large. The organization in coalition with leading business community leaders led an advocacy group in 2010 to successfully repeal the US imposed ban on travel for people with HIV. About a hundred CEOs have signed as part of advocacy group to end workplace stigma and discrimination of people with HIV. Even today, about 45 countries still restrict the entry, stay, or residence of people, based only on their HIV positive status. This means more than 30 million people could be denied entry, deported, or detained by 45 countries. GBC Health, in partnership with UNAIDS and Levi Strauss & Co., is working with the CEOs by securing their right to oppose restrictions on the freedom of movement for people living with HIV. Chip Bergh, president and CEO of Levi Strauss & Co., and Kenneth Cole, CEO of Kenneth Cole Productions and chairman of the board of the foundation for AIDS Research along with CEOs of other companies such as Coca Cola, Johnson

& Johnson, National Basketball Association, Heineken, Pfizer, Aetna, and such others are advocating lifting the ban. These laws and policies violate human rights and don't help public health systems, because people infected with HIV, for fear of being detected, do not carry the pills with them while on travel and skipping HIV medication leads to drug resistance, which is a public health concern. The revolutionary antiretroviral treatment made people with HIV fully productive workers living long and healthy lives. The treatment reduces the amount of HIV in one's body to an undetectable level, lowering the possibility of transmitting HIV to someone else by almost 96 percent. There's no evidence that HIV travel restrictions affects public health, besides stopping people from entering countries harms businesses. In today's competitive landscape, work-related travel is essential for corporations. Companies should be able to send executives overseas regardless of their HIV status.

This is advocacy at the global level, pushing for global reform in protecting human rights and simultaneously interests of corporations. In such cases, governments find it hard to influence other countries. Hence NGOs, industry lobbies, and social advocacy groups come into the picture to help bring in global understanding on a specific issue.

Jody Williams[2,3,4] is an American political activist and in 1997, she won the Nobel Peace Prize for her works in banning and clearing of anti-personnel landmines. Anti-personnel landmines are designed to keep human beings at bay. They are carefully planted just a few inches beneath the ground, not visible to naked eye, and when human beings step on it, the bombs go off. Interestingly, they are designed not to kill, but injure, by damaging the legs, primarily to inflict harm to the larger logistical support the enemy side might need. Often, once the conflict ceases, the landmines are not unearthed or diffused. So subsequently when the bombs go off, they don't recognize whether it is enemy, solider, farmer, child, or whoever. Jody Williams says, 'Landmines distinguish themselves because once they have been sown, once the soldier walks away from the weapon, the landmine cannot tell the difference between a soldier or a civilian, a woman, a child, or a grandmother going out to collect firewood to make a family meal. The landmine is eternally prepared to take victims. It is the perfect soldier, the 'eternal sentry.'

Jody Williams was born in 1950 in Vermont, and at an early age she fought injustice when other children at school were picking on her brother who was deaf and suffered from schizophrenia. She also fought for peace, protesting the war in Vietnam. In 1976, she earned a master's degree in Spanish and English as a Second

Language. After that for two years, she taught in Mexico, where she came across extreme poverty. In 1984, she earned her master's in international relations from Johns Hopkins University. One day she got interested in the war which the US was involved with in El Salvador. She began passionately opposing it. For two years she led delegations as a coordinator of the Nicaragua–Honduras Education Project. Subsequently, she started working on humanitarian relief projects and also served as the deputy director of the organization Medical Aid for El Salvador. Sometime in late 1991, Bobby Muller, president of the Vietnam Veterans of America Foundation, asked Williams if she would be interested in coordinating efforts to ban landmines worldwide. She loved the idea and started mobilizing NGOs to help her with the cause. In October 1992, the International Campaign to Ban Landmines (ICBL) was formally launched and called for a complete ban on use, production, trade, and stockpiling of landmines. As the chief strategist for ICBL, Williams drove the programme by approaching United Nations, the European Parliament, and the Organization of African Unity. Along with co-author Shawn Roberts, she published *After the Guns Fall Silent: The Enduring Legacy of Landmines*. The book explored long term effects of land mines on human life, a tragedy of unparalleled proportions. She advocated that unless landmines are diffused, people cannot work or travel safely and that increases unemployment. Jody Williams once told a reporter, 'People have this idea that landmined fields are set off with barbed wire like they are in Second World War movies, but that is not how it is. They put them where people go. They put them next to watering holes, along the banks of the river, in the fields. It is not realistic for people to stay out of those areas.'

Working without any staff, relying solely on her own efforts, Jody Williams convinced more than 1,000 NGOs from nearly 60 plus countries to support the ICBL campaign. Even Princess Diana participated and visited victims in Angola and Bosnia, which are the world's most heavily landmined countries. In 1996, the Canadian Government agreed to draw up an international treaty banning landmines and in December 1997, the treaty was signed with the support of 122 countries. In recognition for her efforts, Jody Williams and the ICBL became co-recipients of the 1997 Nobel Peace Prize. As of today about 160 countries have signed the landmine ban treaty. Conferring the Nobel Peace Prize, Francis Sejersted, chairman of the Norwegian Nobel Committee said, 'There are those among us who are unswerving in their faith that things can be done to make our world a better, safer, and more humane place and who also, even when the tasks appear overwhelming, have the courage to tackle them. You have helped to rouse public opinion all over the world against the use of an arms technology that strikes quite randomly at the most innocent and most defenseless.' In 2004, *Forbes* magazine named Jody Williams as one of the 100 most powerful women in the world.

Often, advocacy helps people and communities to come together to rally against inhuman situations and tragedies. Uplifting the lives of people and thereby, giving hope to them, is a contribution to humanity. One of the biggest points on the agenda of world, corporate, and community leaders is to be advocates in helping people live their lives, earn their livelihood, banish poverty, establish harmony, and peaceful coexistence. To be a good advocate, one needs to have:

- Passion: A cause that you are passionate about.
- Energy: Energy to drive the cause.
- Perseverance: Persevere until the cause is attained.
- Courage: A fearless attitude to face consequences.
- Influence: Ability to rally and convince people to support the cause.

Advocacy tests the mettle of one's leadership and at times people lose their freedom and are incarcerated too. Between 2003 and 2007, Liu Xiaobo[9] served as president of the Independent Chinese PEN Centre. He is based out of Beijing and is a literary critic, writer, and political activist. He worked as a professor at Beijing Normal University and was a visiting professor at several universities outside of China—University of Oslo, University of Hawaii, and Columbia University, NY. He was awarded the 2009 PEN Barbara Goldsmith Freedom to Write Award and on December 10, 2010, he was awarded the Nobel Peace Prize. But he was not allowed to go to Oslo to receive it because he had been under arrest and kept incommunicado by the Chinese Government.

In the spring of 1989, when Liu returned to Beijing after leaving Columbia University, in support of students, he supported the non-violent pro-democracy movement by staging a hunger strike in Tiananmen Square and called for a sustainable democratic movement. He was arrested and sent to prison for two years. In 1996, he was sent to prison for another three years, for calling for dialogue between the Dalai Lama of Tibet and the Chinese communist government. In 2004, his telephone and Internet connections were disconnected for his writings against the government on how it silences the journalists and activists. He was again arrested on December 8, 2008, along with fellow activist Zhang Zuhua and his computers and other documents were confiscated. His arrest coincided with the 100 year anniversary of China's first constitution. On October 8, 2010, when he was told that he was awarded the Nobel Prize, he wept and said to his wife, Liu Xia, 'The prize is dedicated to the martyrs of Tiananmen Square.'

On December 23, 2009, the People's Court tried Liu, and he pleaded not guilty to the charge of 'inciting subversion of state power', because he co-authored Charter 08, a declaration calling for political reform, greater emphasis on human rights, and an end to single party rule in China. The trial lasted less than three hours, and the defense was not permitted to present evidence. On December 25, Liu was sentenced to 11 years in prison and on February 11, 2010, the Beijing High Court rejected his appeal.

When people try to attempt a systemic change at a global scale, especially effecting the functioning of governments, colossal resistance arising from the ideology of political power can be expected. Often, political advocacy addresses structuring and redistribution of political power, which is unacceptable as it thwarts existing power equations, irrespective of rationality of thought. That is the real challenge any person advocating the cause in change of power has to face with—sustain to make a shift.

Serving as a consumer advocate and an advocate for the American economy, is an integral part of Allstate's[7,8] 78 year heritage. In the 1930s, Allstate was one of the first companies to create a sophisticated rate classification system, giving better rates to safe drivers. In the 1950s, Allstate opened its first drive-in claim office, revolutionizing the way automobile claims are handled. In 1960s, the company helped convince the government to make seat-belt use mandatory, and in the 1970s and 80s, Allstate played an instrumental role in advocating the safety benefits of air-bags.

With revenues at $33.31 billion ending December 30, 2012, and assets nearly at $130 billion, the Allstate Corporation is the largest publicly held personal lines property and casualty insurer in America. In 1933, it became a publicly traded company and as on 2011, it was ranked 93 on the *Fortune* 500 list of largest companies in the US. The company has more than 70,000 professionals comprising of employees, agency owners, and staff. Of the nearly 40,000 employees, 60 percent constitute women, and more than 30 percent are minorities. The company insures close to 17 million households.

On December 2, 2008, Vanessa Williams kicked off Allstate's Safe Teen Driving Campaign by signing the Parent–Teen Contract with her son Devin, where she emphasized the importance of talking to teenage children about safe driving habits such as not using cell phone, not texting, listening to blaring music, not drinking and driving, and such others and avoiding any distractions while behind the wheel.

Allstate is advocating the cause of making 'smart' driving socially acceptable. They are doing this by using the power of peer-to-peer influence. The idea stems from the view that it is teens that can inform and influence each other. In addition, in 2011 it conducted new efforts to help educate the public about the value and importance of stronger teen driving laws, which have been proven to save lives on the road. In the three years starting 2008, 6.3 million teenage children were informed about road safety aspects, nearly 8,50,000 teenagers were involved in projects, contests, and related programmes and about 45,000 teenagers were involved in active projects advocating road safety programmes. Thanks to the advocacy, between 2008 and 2011, there was a 23 percent reduction in teenage deaths on US roads from 4,070 in 2008 to 3,115 in 2010.

Advocacy often is about informing, influencing, and helping people realize the right thing to do. Many parents find it difficult to educate or drive sense into their teenage children because of the transitional gap both of them experience at that age. The only people who can influence teens are teens themselves. There is no one strategy that fits all. Different methods of influence have to be used while advocating a cause.

Aamir Khan is one of India's biggest movie stars and his TV show 'Satyamev Jayte' focused on social issues. He was featured on *Time* magazine cover (April 29–May 6, 2013) as one of the 100 most influential people in the world. Academy award winner and Music Composer, A.R. Rahman writes on Aamir Khan, 'His TV show is part journalism, part talk show, and it confronts India's deepest social ills, from sexual abuse to caste discrimination. He uses his gift as a charmer to give the audience the most, bitter medicine. Hypnotized, we take it without a complaint... 'Satyamev Jayate', was not intended to provide solutions, but to ask the hard questions, the kind society is often reluctant to address. By showing the courage to ask those questions, Aamir has started a movement that will help change the world in which Indians live. Jai ho!' The platform for advocacy also changes from addressing grassroot issues to addressing issues where mindsets have to change. Depending upon the influencing capabilities of the advocate, the platform can spring forth energy that can sway a community or a nation. Importantly, advocacy is not always about coming out with solutions. Solutions emerge when there is awareness. Steeped in ancient traditions, when people are reluctant to change with times, advocacy is perhaps the only tool that can help influence and change the mindsets, to enable people to rethink about obsolete traditions and customs.

Malala[1] (grief-stricken) Yousafzai was born in July 1997 into a Muslim family of Pashtun ethnicity in Pakistan, and lived in Mingora. Her father Ziauddin Yousafzai is a poet, school owner, and an educational activist and runs Khushal Public Schools, a chain of schools. At 11, young Malala started to speak about education rights and in her speech at Peshawar, she added, 'How dare the Taliban take away my basic right to education?' This was covered by newspapers and television channels throughout the region. Around the same time Maulana Fazlullah was leading the Taliban in swat valley and as per Taliban dictum, watching television, listening to music, and education for girls are banned. In line with this edict, Taliban had already destroyed more than 100 schools attended by girls.

Meanwhile, Abdul Hai Kakkar, a BBC reporter in Pakistan approached Malala's father, asking whether any woman from his school was willing to write about experiences about leading life under Taliban. A girl named Aisha came forward, but was stopped by her parents, out of fear for the Taliban. That is when Malala, who was in seventh grade, agreed to write and BBC agreed. On January 3, 2009, BBC posted her blog—'I had a terrible dream yesterday about military helicopters and the Taliban. I have had such dreams since the launch of the military operation in Swat. My mother made me breakfast and I went off to school. I was afraid of going to school because the Taliban had issued an edict banning all girls from attending school. Only 11 girls attended the class out of 27. The number decreased because of Taliban's edict. My three friends have shifted to Peshawar, Lahore, and Rawalpindi with their families after this edict. On my way from school to home, I heard a man saying, "I will kill you." I hastened my pace and after a while I looked back if the man was still coming behind me. But to my utter relief he was talking on his mobile and must have been threatening someone else over the phone.'

And her blogs continued about her thoughts, views, and life in the months. Soon, the BBC diary ended and Adam B. Ellick, a *New York Times* reporter, approached Malala's father about filming a documentary. Soon, she was interviewed for various channels such as AVT Kyber, Aaj Daily, and Canada's Toronto star. On August 19, 2009 she spoke about wanting to become a politician and named Benazir Bhutto as her inspiration. In the same year, in December, she participated in the Institute for War and Peace Reporting's Open Minds programme, a project that provided journalism training to 42 schools in Pakistan. In October 2011, Desmond Tutu announced Malala's nomination for the International Children's Peace Prize and she became a celebrity. Soon death threats followed and in a meeting held by the Taliban sometime in the summer of 2012, the leaders agreed to kill her.

On October 9, 2012, when Malala was taking a bus ride

to go home, a masked gunman climbed in and shouted, 'Which one of you is Malala? Speak up; otherwise I will shoot you all.' Once identified, she was shot. She was airlifted to Peshawar and after a three hour operation; doctors at the military hospital removed the bullets. Ehsanullah Ehsan, spoke on behalf of the Pakistani Taliban, claimed responsibility and said that she is the symbol of the infidels and obscenity, and that if she survived, they would target her again. On October 15, she was moved to Queen Elizabeth Hospital in Birmingham, UK, for further treatment. It took her three years to recover and on October 18, 2012 BBC announced that Malala had recuperated enough and had become medically fit enough to stand. In February 2013, she went through a five hour operation again to reconstruct her skull.

About the shooting, President Obama said, 'It is reprehensible, disgusting, and tragic.' Gordon Brown, former British prime minister and UN special envoy for Global Education launched a petition using the slogan, 'I am Malala' and demanded that all children globally, should get schooling, by 2015. The public outcry worldwide was unanimous. 14-year-old Malala wrote blogs, talked about education for girls, and she was shot. Advocacy is not easy. Following a cause through its natural course comes with its own perils and needs courage to stand up to despite the brutalities of life.

Advocacy changes the way people think and perceive the world around them. For a better world, it is important to take up causes, which you are passionate about. What you stand for is more important, and not how small or big the cause is.

Philanthropy

'What we have done for ourselves alone dies with us; what we have done for others and the world remains and is immortal.'

—Albert Pike

PHILANTHROPY ACTUALLY MEANS LOVE for humanity and is conventionally defined as 'private initiatives, for public good, focusing on quality of life.'

Many in the world, for the love of humanity, irrespective of being rich or poor, have focused on philanthropic initiatives concerning poverty, education, health, and other such social aspects. Giving back to the community is important because it enriches the brotherhood of mankind, makes you feel like a part of a larger fabric of human existence and, develops a deep sense of sensitivity towards others. Many CEOs, corporate chieftains, politicians, investors, and others have contributed to philanthropic activities to help alleviate the quality of life. Some have donated to social causes; some went about creating trusts, charitable and educational institutions, while a few created lasting impact by contributing their time, effort, money, and other resources to the creation of world-class universities.

Harvard University[1] was established in 1636 by vote of the Great and General Court of the Massachusetts Bay Colony, making it the oldest institution of higher learning in the US. It was initially called the 'New College' and was renamed Harvard College on March 13, 1639, after an English clergyman from Southwark, London, an alumnus of the University of Cambridge, because he bequeathed his library of 400 books and 779 Pound Sterling, which was at that time, half his estate. Today the main campus of Harvard is 210 acres; the University endowment fund is perhaps the largest in the world at $32 billion. Eight US Presidents have been graduates of this University, 75 Nobel Laureates have been attatched as students, faculty, or associates, and the University is alma mater to about 62 living billionaires.

Leland Stanford[2], studied law in New York and then moved westward, after the gold rush. Like many of his contemporaries, he also made a fortune in the railroad business. He then became the leader of the Republican Party, subsequently governor of California and later a US

Senator. He and his wife Jane had a son, Leland Stanford Junior, who in the year 1884, died of typhoid when the family was travelling to Florence, Italy. After his death, the Stanfords decided that the children of California shall be their children and in the memory of their son, they donated their wealth by creating an educational institution. After six years of planning and construction, on October 1, 1891, Stanford University opened its doors. The first student body consisted of 555 men and women, and by the second year, the faculty had expanded to 49 people. The endowment of the university stands at $17 billion and 19 Nobel Laureates are members of the Stanford Community.

The MIT Sloan School of Management[3] was founded in 1914, and a master's degree in management was established in 1925. The Sloan fellowship programme was created in 1931 under the aegis of Alfred P. Sloan, a MIT graduate himself and the chairman of General Motors. The school of Industrial Management was established in 1952 from the Alfred P, Sloan Foundation grant. The endowment of Sloan School of Management stands at nearly $700 million and is one of the most sought after schools in the world for management studies. Notable Alumni include

Nobel Laureate Robert Solow, for his contributions to the theory of economic growth, CEO of Ford, Alan Mulally, Carly Fiorina, CEO of HP, Kofi Annan, general secretary of UN, and Benjamin Netanyahu, prime minister of Isreal.

Andrew Dickson White of Syracuse and Ezra Cornell of Ithaca founded Cornell University in 1865. The University was initially funded by Ezra Cornell's $4,00,000 endowment. Cornell had great regard for philanthropy for the purpose of education and desired to use the endowment 'to do the greatest good'. Cornell who was poor for most of his life, earned money through self education and sheer hard work. He wanted to do something of great value with the money he earned and he wrote, 'My greatest care now is how to spend this large income to do the greatest good to those who are properly dependent on me, to the poor and to posterity.' Andrew Dickson White went to Geneva Academy, where he learnt about Oxford University and University of Cambridge. He dreamt of a University worthy of the commonwealth and of the nation and subsequently, along with Ezra Cornell helped create the foundation for Cornell University. The University's current endowment stands at nearly $5.5 billion, and its alumni constitute 31 Marshall and 28 Rhodes scholars. Notable alumni include Lee Teng Hui, president of Taiwan; Mario Garcia Menocal, president of Cuba; Jamshid Amuzegar, prime minister of Iran; Hu Shih, Chinese reformer and representative of United

Nations. In addition, notable faculty include people like Norman Borlaug, father of the green revolution and Georgios Papanikolaou, inventor of the pap smear test to detect cervical cancer.

Philanthropy is not just about donating wealth; it needs a vision to create a society with intellect. In my view, the four pillars of any intellect-driven society are: higher education, economic growth, healthy citizens, and effective governance.

Manoj Bhargava[10], CEO of 5-hour Energy; a company that markets the caffeine based stimulant drinks. According to *Forbes* magazine, in 2012, Bhargava may be the wealthiest Indian in America. As on March 2013, his estimated net worth is $3 billion. Bhargava was awarded, Crain's Detroit Business' 'Newsmaker of the Year 2011' award and he was named Ernst & Young's Entrepreneur of the Year for 2012. Bhargava joined 'Giving Pledge', which was started by Bill and Melinda Gates, together with Warren Buffet, in June 2010. The programme is an effort to get America's and the world's wealthiest people to give away at least 50 percent of their wealth during their lifetimes, or upon death, and write a letter explaining why. Here is Manoj Bhargava's letter.

> 'My choice was to ruin my son's life giving him money or giving 90+ percent to charity. Not much of a choice. Service to others seems the only intelligent choice for

the use of wealth. The other choices especially personal consumption seems either useless or harmful.

This projects that our foundation works are defined only as alleviating human suffering. We have adopted over 400 charities from schools and hospitals to women's career and education in rural India. We are also working on desalinating water cheaply, reducing fossil fuel emissions by 50 percent, cleaning mercury and sulfur dioxide from coal, and a revolutionary medical technology that will improve overall health for the poor and the not so poor.

For us, all of this falls under reducing human suffering. We may not be able to affect human suffering on a grand scale but it will be fun trying.'

The Rockefeller Foundation[11] has completed a century of philanthropic activities. Here are interesting excerpts from the documented history of the foundation and the impact it made from its website, www.rockfellerfoundation.org. '...On April 24, 1913, The New York state legislature passed an act incorporating the Rockefeller Foundation with the statement of purpose reading: "To promote the well-being of mankind throughout the world." John D. Rockefeller Sr makes a gift to the Foundation totaling $35 million, and followed it with another grant of $65 million in 1913.'

On December 5, 1913, the Foundation makes its first

grant of $100,000 to the American Red Cross to purchase property for its headquarters in Washington, DC, and for 'a memorial to commemorate the services of the women of the US in caring for the sick and wounded of the Civil War'. In 1917, the Foundation established the Peking Union Medical College, for pre-medical students. It was referred to as the 'John Hopkins of China'. In 1918, after the First World War ended, the foundation spent upwards of $22 million sending food supplies to Belgium, Poland, Serbia, Armenia, and other affected countries. Between 1921 and 1941, the foundation spent over $ 25 million to establish schools in Prague, Warsaw, London, Toronto, Copenhagen, Budapest, Oslo, Belgrade, Zagreb, Madrid, Cluj (Romania), Ankara, Sofia, Rome, Tokyo, Athens, Bucharest, Stockholm, Calcutta, Manila and São Paulo. Between 1933 and 1953, the Foundation spent $1.5 million in identifying and assisting 300 scientists and scholars fleeing Nazi Germany to settle in friendly locations as well as relocate to US universities. In 1950, Max Theiler of the Foundation's Virus Laboratory in New York City won the Nobel Prize in medicine and physiology for developing the yellow fever vaccine. In 1960, The International Rice Research Institute, the first of what became a system of 16 international agricultural centres, was established in the Philippines. In 1970, The Nobel Peace Prize was awarded to Dr Norman E. Borlaug, a foundation agricultural scientist, for his pivotal role in modernizing agriculture (green revolution) in the developing world. In 1992, The Population Sciences programme initiated a 10-year programme to make quality family planning and reproductive health available to every couple in the world that wants it. In 2005, the Foundation commited $3 million for housing and economic redevelopment in response to hurricane Katrina.'

Here is the letter by David Rockefeller titled 'Philanthropic Pledge' as a part of the Giving Pledge effort.

> '...In the end (philanthropic) success requires much more than financial resources, although money is, of course essential. Good ideas are just as important; otherwise one risks wasting both the funds and the opportunity. Effective philanthropy also requires patience–patience to deal with unexpected obstacles; patience to wait for the first, slight stirrings of change; and patience to listen to the insights and ideas of others.
>
> For five generations, my family has experienced the real satisfaction and pleasure of philanthropy. Our engagement has helped create a strong group of institutions, including the University of Chicago, The Rockefeller University, the museum of modern art, the Rockefeller Brothers Fund. The practice of philanthropy also has enables many of us to become personally involved in efforts to address critical

> global challenges such as poverty, health, sustainable development, and environmental degradation...'

Both Manoj Bhargava's and David Rockefeller's letters are self-explanatory. Philanthropy becomes a way of life, a natural choice for the wealthy to exercise. Instead of degenerating progeny with inherited wealth, these pioneers are creating foundations of service, in the hope that these institutions will help establish life goals for the next generation and the generations thereafter to serve humanity. People have been smart enough to realize that consumption of personal wealth beyond accustomed lifestyle is either useless or harmful.

Warren Buffet[9], the world's richest person, a prudent American investor, with an estimated wealth of $55 billion as on early 2013, is giving away 99 percent of his wealth, 83 percent of which will go to the Bill and Melinda Gates Foundation. He will be remembered more for philanthropy than for anything else. In 1988, he expressed his thoughts of reallocating wealth, 'I don't have a problem with guilt about money. The way I see it is that my money represents an enormous number of claim checks on society. It's like I have these little pieces of paper that I can turn into consumption. If I wanted to, I could hire 10,000 people to do nothing but paint my picture every day for the rest of my life. And the GDP would go up. But the utility of the product would be zilch, and I would be keeping those 10,000 people from doing AIDS research, or teaching, or nursing. I don't do that though. I don't use very many of those claim checks. There's nothing material I want very much. And I'm going to give virtually all of those claim checks to charity when my wife and I die.'

Buffet doesn't believe in the concept of inherited wealth and calls those who had that good fortune, 'members of a lucky sperm club'. About passing on wealth to his children, he said, 'I want to give my kids just enough so that they would feel that they could do anything, but not so much that they would feel like doing nothing.'

Here is an excerpt of Buffet's letter as part of the Giving Pledge initiative:

> '...More than 99% of my wealth will go to philanthropy during my lifetime or at death. Measured by dollars, this commitment is large. In a comparative sense, though, many individuals give more to others every day.
>
> Millions of people who regularly contribute to churches, schools, and other organizations thereby relinquish the use of funds that would otherwise benefit their own families. The dollars these people drop into a collection plate or give to United Way mean forgone movies, dinners out, or other personal pleasures. In contrast, my family and I will give up nothing we need or want by fulfilling this 99 precent pledge.

> Moreover, this pledge does not leave me contributing the most precious asset, which is time. Many people, including—I am proud to say, my three children, give extensively of their own time and talents to help others. Gifts of this kind often prove far more valuable than money. A struggling child, befriended and nurtured by a caring mentor, receives a gift whose value far exceeds what can be bestowed by a check. My sister, Doris, extends significant person-to-person help daily. I have done little of this...'

Importantly, despite his vast wealth, Warren Buffet seems to have inculcated the values of 'gifting and contributing to humanity' into his three children. Interestingly, he values 'time' over 'money' as the true measure of contribution. Often people use time in self-pursuit or self-indulgence, and hardly towards activities that help fellow human beings or in community activities. True intellect driven leadership is attained only when people understand this fundamental principle—leadership is about building communities and developing people.

When writing about philanthropy, it would be unfair not to write about Bill and Melinda Gates[10], and what they are doing for human betterment. In the annals of history, Bill Gates will perhaps be remembered more for his foundation work than for founding Microsoft. The foundation they set up is into venture philanthropy, which combines venture capital principles and high tech approaches to accomplishing philanthropic goals. Bill and Melinda write, 'Our friend and co-trustee Warren Buffet once gave us some great advice about philanthropy—"Don't just go for safe projects, take on the really tough problems," and that is exactly what the foundation does.' With an asset trust endowment at $36.4 billion, which is more than 50 percent of Bill Gate's wealth, 1,116 employees, supporting 50 states in the US and a 100 countries, the Foundation, the largest in the world, works on uplifting humanity. Both Bill and Melinda believe that some of the projects they fund, would fail, and expect it too, because they think that 'the essential role of philanthropy is to make bets on promising solutions that governments and businesses can't afford to make'.

An excerpt from Bill and Melinda Gates letter, as part of the Giving Pledge effort:

> '...Both of us were fortunate to grow up with parents who taught us some tremendously important values. Work hard. Show respect. Have a sense of humor. And if life happens to bless you with talent or treasure, you have a responsibility to use those gifts as well and as wisely as you possibly can. Now we hope to pass this example on to our own children...'

As on April 2013, Azim Premji[10], chairman of the $7.5 billion Wipro Corporation said that he has donated almost 25 percent of his wealth to charity and is the first Indian and the third person outside the US, after Richard Branson and David Sainsbury to join the Giving Pledge effort, where he has made a pledge to dedicate a substantial portion of his wealth for philanthropic purposes. More importantly he founded the Azim Premji Foundation by donating $2 billion of his personal wealth. The foundation works in developing primary education, and the goal is to create a just, equitable, humane, and sustainable society in India.

The fundamental nature of philanthropy is to 'give' and many world leaders realize that true redemption is not in acquisition of wealth, but in giving away wealth for bettering human life. All these people are driven by a fundamental value system of serving humanity. Importantly, all of them recognize that distribution of wealth in the hands of many has more use than concentrating it in a few hands. Besides, wealth beyond a threshold is a big overhead, at times possessing the possessor and not necessarily offering the happiness or the hope associated with it.

Learn to give, that is the only way to lead a happier and enriching life.

Diversity

'Strength lies in differences, not in similarities.'

—Stephen R. Covey

THE WORLD IS GLOBALIZED, what happens in one part of the world, affects the remotest corner of the planet. As I meet, consult, and talk to senior executives, the biggest challenge I encounter is people's ability to work in diverse environments. Often business opportunities face the brunt of inability of people to work with people of other cultures and engage with thinking of people with diverse views. We seem to bask in minor successes emanating from similarities, but in reality are missing out on the big opportunities that come with enmeshing with diversity. A CEO who I recently met said, 'Our products are no more regional. Help us find people who have worked on global initiatives and who can easily engage with people of various nationalities.' Another senior executive couldn't get to the next level because she didn't understand what it takes to work in diverse work groups. Corporations transcend physical boundaries and are looking for market opportunities where there is a consumer who is willing to spend. And this consumer is a product of his or her own culture and has choices galore. Coming to think of choice, Sweden alone has upwards of fifty newspapers. So, how does one work with people with different mindsets who make choices and decisions based on individual preferences? There is diversity of thought, products, services, culture, customs, traditions, and norms. Diversity is about wading through this complex network of human behaviour with a deep sense of understanding of what it takes to collaborate. In diverse collaborations lies the future of products and success.

John Chambers, chairman and CEO of CISCO[1,2,3] says, 'When we talk about diversity at CISCO, it's about inclusion—bringing together a diverse workforce with unique life experiences, cultures, talents, and perspectives. We promote a creative, innovative, and collaborative environment that helps drive our business strategy.' CISCO has been on the Working Mother 100 Best Companies for four consecutive years from 2008 onwards. WorkingMother.com states, 'Cisco has two onsite childcare centres, offering holiday and vacation care and an eleven week summer camp for employee's children between ages 6 and 12. In addition, Cisco has a very generous leave policy, where employees receive at least twenty days of paid time off per year, plus ten paid holidays and one floating holiday. Besides, it takes just twenty hours of work per week to earn medical insurance, which encourages the use of flexible schedules, and there's free health coaching, six onsite gyms and a medical centre with a pharmacy at the headquarters. Workers and their families can use the employee assistance programme to arrange free sessions with legal and financial experts, talk to a counsellor or meet with a college coach. If they find themselves facing tough times financially, they may apply to the Family Crisis Assistance Programme for one-time payouts of around $2,000 to $5,000.'

Very few companies recognize what it takes to leverage the talent and commitment of working mothers, who juggle multiple schedules between home, office, and their children. Most women live a 36 hour day in every 24 hours. World class companies that offer flexibility and resources to working moms live the concept of diversity and enhance employee morale significantly.

Here is another interesting case of diversity of thought. In 2005, McDonald's (UK) allowed its employees to share their job with family members. The family contract policy allowed family members over 16 years of age viz., children, spouses, and grandparents to share jobs by swapping the shifts without notifying McDonald's management. As per the contract, which was the first of its kind in UK, based on who clocks how many hours, each of them is paid separately through his or her own bank account. This policy applies to cohabiting and same sex partners as well, and McDonald's was also looking at extending its benefits to friends and extended family. David Fairhurst, the head of McDonald's UK human resources operation, said, 'A lot of our staff wanted more flexibility. Many are youngsters at college who have very different term hours and holiday hours. Many older staff have children, with all the demands that entails. Many look after relatives. So we decided to offer them the flexibility in a family context.' This flexibility is a big win for McDonald's because it enhanced diversity and reduced the number of sick days, besides this programme was supported by the Department of Trade and Industry. 42-year-old Rita Cross was the first to sign up along with her two daughters Laura (18) and Natalie (16). Laura says, 'We get up in the morning and decide which of us really wants to go to work.'

On November 29, 2012, *The New York Times*, published an article titled, 'The Autism Advantage'. Thorkil Sonne and his wife Annette realized that their son Lars was a high functioning autistic, who was extremely detail oriented. When Lars was 7, the family had gone on a long car trip from Scotland to Germany, and Lars passed time in the back seat studying a road atlas. On his return from the trip, Lars drew rectangles and inserted numerals into them, sketching the map of Europe. When Sonne picked up the road atlas and compared the numerals to the page numbers listed in the boxes for each country, he noticed that all the numbers perfectly matched and he was stunned. Sonne discovered that Lars had an unusual skill of intense focus and careful execution, a skill, as technical director of TDS, Denmark's largest telecommunications company, he sought from each of his employees. Hearing similar stories from parents and other autism organizations, he conceived a business plan to engage high functioning autistic people to perform specific and tedious tasks such as data entry or software testing, which many autistic people are exceptionally good at. In 2003, Sonne quit his job, mortgaged the home, took a crash course on accounting, and started a company named, Specialisterne (Danish for 'the specialists'). The company employed 35 high functioning autistic workers as consultants and serviced 19 companies in Denmark. The World Economic Forum meeting took place in Tianjin in September 2012, and Sonne was named one of 26 winners of a global social entrepreneurship awards. Specialisterne has inspired start-ups and has five of its own, around the world. 'He has made me think about this differently, that these individuals can be a part of our business and our plans,' says Ernie Dianastasis, managing director of CAI, an information technology company that has agreed to work with Specialisterne to find jobs for autistic software testers in the US. A woman from Hawaii wrote to Sonne asking whether she could move to Denmark to enable her unemployed autistic child to join the Specialisterne team. The emerging understanding of the autistic mind will unfold many opportunities in the future. However, considering the need of autistic people for predictive work environments, it would pose a different challenge altogether for standard work places conceived for paranormals.

To this end, SAP[7], one of the world's largest enterprise software product development companies, has a strategic vision to focus on the unique abilities that everyone brings to the table. It recently launched a global collaboration with Specialisterne to employ people with autism in best-fit roles such as software testing. SAP's goal is to globally employ and engage about 1 percent of its 65,000 employees with autism by the year 2020. 'At SAP, we see diversity and inclusion as a competitive advantage,' says Anka Wittenberg, SAP's chief diversity and inclusion officer. The *Guardian*, in its May 22, 2013, article reported that: 'Melanie Altrock, 27, who has Asperger's, spoke of her relief at having found work after a Berlin company, Auticon which specializes in finding IT roles for people with the condition, took her on. She said she had spent years moving from one low-paid job to another, knowing she had more to offer. "Even my psychiatrist told me that he wouldn't employ me. And I know you just have to look at me to know that I'm different and don't fit into the normal workplace," she told German radio. Now she works as a software tester where her memory skills and attention to detail are highly valuable. "Finally I feel I have something to offer," she said.'

Inclusion is not about just providing means of livelihood, it is also about providing social security. True inclusion is when we make all sections of the society feel wanted. The starting point of inclusion is when we value what people have to offer, recognize their work, and develop competencies for employability. The essence of human life lies is being rightly valued for the work performed, which raises dignity and self-respect.

Often people associate diversity with equitable opportunities relating to—region, religion, gender, sexual preferences, age, and such others—which is fine and a sign of an inclusive, innovative, and holistic growth mindset. However, it is important to note that diversity is about 'positive acceptance and active engagement' at both levels—thought and deed, and in whatever forms and mediums it comes from and that needs inclusivity of all kinds. The real problem with diversity is not that people don't understand or recognize it, but because people are too caught up with the day-to-day business to actively pursue it as an important goal.

Diversity Inc.'s CEO Luke Visconti interviewed Mark Ng, vice president and LGBT (Lesbian Gay Bisexual Transgender) segment manager of Wells Fargo's[6] strategy segment division. Wells Fargo is an American MNC in the financial services domain, having operations across the globe. Ending 2012, its revenues were $86.08 billion with an operating income of $28.47 billion. When the interview started, Luke posed his first question, 'Why has outreach to the LGBT community been such a priority for Wells Fargo?' and Ng replied, 'At one time our outreach to the LGBT market was because it is the right thing to do, because it is part of our overall visions of diversity—which still holds true. But the right answer now is because it's imperative, just like with all the other segments, to our business. A lot of corporations, not only Wells Fargo, are really waking up to the fact that this is a segment that is affluent, profitable, loyal, and has really, really stepped up in terms of responding to corporations holistically and authentically targeting them.'

In response to Visconti's question relating to Asian Outreach programme, Nancy Wong, senior vice president and integrated marketing manager for the Asian Segment in Enterprise Marketing at Wells Fargo says that immigrants are entrepreneurial and many are business owners and Wells Fargo serves the Asian community by focusing on the financials needs of the Asian businesses by developing programmes that help the small business community. Many of these businesses have connections across Asia and have transpacific characteristics, so Wells Fargo designs and offers specific products and services such as treasury management, trade finance, and APEC (Asia-Pacific Economic Cooperation).

Ng adds that John Stumpf, CEO of Wells Fargo, has made it very clear from the beginning that not only LGBT; not only the ethnic segments, but people with disabilities, women, and all these groups really constitute the vision of diversity and they count in the overall diversity programme. Interestingly, Wells Fargo's business strategy is enmeshed with the diversity strategy and the Pride Outreach programme was conceived by Wells Fargo to work with the LGBT group. Having a diversity strategy integrated with overall business strategy delivers much better financial results. Secondly, John Stumpf's overarching vision to integrate diversity with business strategy is perhaps the best method to give wings to diversity initiatives.

While researching for this book, I stumbled upon the name 85 Broads[4] and its uniqueness stuck to me. I decided to figure out what they were about. It is a global network of 30,000 women in 90 countries with 40 professional regional chapters worldwide working both for profit and non-profit organizations. Over a decade, they have enrolled women, who are alumnae and students of world's leading universities, colleges, and schools. The enrollment consists of women from all walks of life—entrepreneurs, investment bankers, consultants, filmmakers, bloggers, lawyers, educators, athletes, venture capitalists, portfolio managers, political leaders, philanthropists, doctors, engineers, artists, scientists, students, and such others. These women engage and invest in each other, shaping thoughts, views, leadership skills, managerial competencies, wealth management, seminars, and other such networking events. Interestingly, the name 85 Broads came from the initial founders who worked for Goldman Sacs at its 85 Broad Street, NYC Headquarters. This perhaps is one of the largest diversity networks that unfolded unfathomable opportunities to women from all walks of life—either in enriching their lives or careers. There is active involvement, participation, and engagement from women across diverse work places, continents, regions, ethnic backgrounds etc. And the ideas of starting something of this nature is incredibly innovative—a global diversity programme cutting across all lines of thought.

Kraft Foods[91] has a jumpstart developmental training programme for new employees, which started in 2003.

It helps with an on board programme for new hires with emphasis on Blacks, Asians, Latinos, and women. The programme, introduces new employees to Kraft's organization culture, the importance of organization building through diversity and inclusion through skill building at various stages of development. Interestingly, the programme touches upon unwritten rules that make people from under-represented groups to leave the organization and this has resulted in improvement in retention of new employees. Kraft's mentoring programme is unique in the sense that more than 70 percent of the pairings are cross-cultural and mentors receive cultural awareness training,

John Lechleiter, chairman, president, and CEO of Eli Lilly and Company said, 'Helping employees integrate work and life is more important than ever as we look for ways to continuously improve productivity… Early in my tenure as a CEO, I made a decision to cut back on our flexible work programmes, and our employee engagement suffered… Bringing these programmes back is one of the best decisions I've made.' Eli Lilly offers many programmes globally—flexible work arrangements, personal leaves, fitness centres, childcare, campus dry cleaners, and family support programmes, which help employees maintain work-life flexibility.

US Black Engineers (USBE) & IT (Information Technology) magazine of April 2011 cites that, as per a survey, the number of supporters has increased for Historically Black colleges and Universities (HBCUs) and part of the reason is attributed to President Obama's focus on supporting the need for more technical talent. He said, 'The Government will increase its funding for the nation's HBCUs by $100 million in the fiscal 2011 budget.' Besides Federal Pell grants of nearly $400 million go to students attending Black institutions. According to President Obama, the survival of HBCUs is vital to achieve the goal of making America the world leader in college graduates by 2020. He said, 'We are not only doing this because these schools are a gateway to a better future for African–Americans. We are doing it because their success is vital to a better future for all Americans.'

Diversity programmes and support is needed at all levels starting from homes, family support, healthcare, schooling, and education, private, corporate, government sectors and non-profit. A diverse workforce, with diverse ideas, and similarities and differences creates a truly enriching experience.

As reported on its website, Boeing supports affinity groups that are employee led associations designed to further personal and professional development, promote diversity within the company, and strengthen networking. The members share a common interest such as race, gender, or cultural identity. The seven affinity groups mentioned below, collectively have more than 80 local chapters

- Boeing American–Indian Society
- Boeing Asian-American Professional Association
- Boeing Black Employees Association
- Boeing Employees Ability Awareness Association
- Boeing Employees Veterans Association
- Boeing Association of Gay, Lesbian, Bi, Transgender Employees & Friends
- Boeing Hispanic Employees Network
- Boeing Women in Leadership

Local diversity representatives support the affinity group and membership is open to all the employees.

Global companies have taken diversity programmes to a new level of inclusiveness, using of people from various backgrounds. Essentially it fosters a behaviour of collaboration and understanding of each other's similarities and differences, and how to respect and work through them. Engaging people from varied cultures makes a significant difference to the way products and services are designed for deployment globally. What works for America, however, may not work everywhere. Cars designed with low ground clearance for the developed markets like the US or Japan, won't work in Bangalore, India, which is known for its bumpy roads. So before launching cars into the Indian market, Toyota asked its Japanese engineers to do test drives along with

Indian engineers and local tour guides to understand the topology and road conditions and accordingly the ground clearance of cars was redesigned. Diverse teams help build personalized services and products for a diverse non-standard world.

SPARC BC's Diversity Project reports that, SAP Global Diversity programmes run some interesting workshops for managers:

- Managing across generations—including Gen Y and new graduates.
- Men and women maximizing the potential of diversity.
- How to innovate and support culturally diverse teams.

These workshops provide learning opportunities for managers to help manage different groups of people from across genders, different cultural groups, and generations. In turn the managers are expected to educate their staff on diversity and inclusive best practices.

Let me end this chapter with a quote from the world famous speech, 'I have a dream' of Rev. Martin Luther King, delivered on August 28, 1963, at the Lincoln Memorial, Washington DC:

'...I have a dream that my four little children will one day live in a nation where they will not be judged by the colour of their skin but by the content of their character....

... I have a dream that one day every valley shall be exalted, and every hill and mountain shall be made low, the rough places will be made plain, and the crooked places will be made straight; and the glory of the Lord shall be revealed and all flesh shall see it together...

....And when this happens, and when we allow freedom ring, when we let it ring from every village and every hamlet, from every state and every city, we will be able to speed up that day when all of God's children, black men and white men, Jews and Gentiles, Protestants and Catholics, will be able to join hands and sing in the words of the old Negro spiritual:

Free at last! Free at last!
Thank God Almighty, we are free at last!...'

Rev. Martin Luther King's speech is nothing but a call for freedom for the black people to be integrated into the soul of the American nation, to be treated as any other white citizen—fair and square. It was a cry for 'inclusion'! History and philosophy of life are replete with examples of importance of diversity and inclusion. All one has to do is to embrace it with an open mind.

SITUATIONAL LEADERSHIP

'A leader is best when people barely know he exists,
when his work is done, his aim fulfilled, they will say:
we did it ourselves.'

—**Lao Tzu**

LEADERSHIP IS PERHAPS ONE of the most researched subjects and the definition of a leader ranges from somebody who energizes, shows vision, and translates it to reality, to raising the bar on standards of excellence, somebody who leads, follows, rallies for a common purpose, has inner strength, shows hope, has no title, obeys, commands, produces leaders, influences, has high personal standards, takes ordinary to extraordinary, innovates, sets rules, engages in details, is an integrator, simplifies, is focused, takes charge and responsibility that comes with it, and leads in chaos. And if we dig deeper, some more qualities also flow in, such as being a good listener, quiet, energetic, team worker, skillful negotiator, artful presenter, emotionally strong, and good with people.

All of the above could be true and depending on how people have excelled in varied fields such as business, economics, academics, politics, and social service amongst others, a definition of leadership has cropped up. That is fine because that is how research fathoms depth of thought, is evidence driven and precise. However, in a rapidly changing world, precision too is dynamic and is determined by context and people who are constantly leaping on to the next. So, leadership tends to be both precise and generic, and at the same time a paradox that we have to learn to thrive in.

Austrian physicist Erwin Schrodinger[3], in 1935 conducted the famous thought experiment—a cat, a flask of poison, and a radioactive substance are placed in a sealed box. If the monitor inside the box detects radioactivity, the flask breaks and releases the poison that kills the cat. Now, for an observer, 'Is the cat dead or alive?' Copenhagen interpretation of quantum mechanics says that the cat is simultaneously alive and dead. However, when you open the box, the cat is alive or dead and not both alive and dead. This poses the question of when exactly does quantum super position end and reality evoke the possibility of one choice over the other.

Similarly, if we look at the cat experiment, the number

of variables in leadership dimension is so many, that to determine the impact, all of them almost converge simultaneously, but when reality unfolds, the factors kind of narrows down to a choice based on the context (markets, technologies) and people involved (emotional, cognitive, and technical capabilities). Simply put, as I see it from a sheer practitioner's viewpoint, I lean more towards Fielder's contingent theory, which states that there is no best way to lead a company, or to make decisions, instead the best course of action is contingent upon internal and external situations. But then I kind of narrow it down to two core dimensions of context and people, constantly evolving upon the collective learning of humanity. Besides, given the rapidly changing world, with unfathomable human complexity, where events are falling upon each other, unfolding with phenomenal rapidity, context is always a flux and people are swirling in the information explosion.

In such a situation, dealing with ambiguity and flux induces shorter shelf lives for leaders. Everybody has a shelf life and that is the Peter Principle of reaching one's highest level of incompetence. January–February, 2013 issue of *Harvard Business Review* states, 'There is a considerable turnover in the top hundred CEOs with 43 percent new on the list compared to 2010,' perhaps owing to the fact that the sample coverage included more global CEOs. Interestingly, the majority of the new entrants to the top CEOs list are from emerging markets. Research has proven that what drives founders initially does not necessarily work for the next growth phase. But most founders find it extremely difficult to cede and make space for the next set of leaders for three reasons. Firstly, they are emotionally attached to their companies and cannot let go, secondly they don't have a second life story and do not know what to do when their existence becomes irrelevant in the company, and lastly, most of them are still basking in the glory and sunshine of yesteryears. So they end up promoting themselves to leadership positions, while the market surpasses them.

On the flipside, there are founders like Mark Zukerberg who became the CEO of Facebook at 22 and quickly learnt the ropes and started to mature as a leader and is now leading the company much more effectively. It is a combination of situation and personal ability. Scalability, I believe, is a dynamic factor, some leaders can and some just can't adapt to it. Similarly, research clearly states that it takes a different leadership style to turn around a company, fix products and services or innovate, and a different one to lead it to the next phase of growth. In a nutshell, different times, different companies, depending upon context, need different kind of leaders at different stages of its evolution and when leaders step in, they bring in their personalities and other dimensions, based on their visioning, people management ability, decision making, and other such capabilities. The impact that a leader and his personality has on establishments is equally proportional. As much as companies, communities and countries create leaders, the style of leadership and the leader's personality too has an equal impact on the evolution of these establishments. But on the leadership front, when it comes to people, the dimension of emotional intelligence seems to be an underlying common denominator for any leader and this aspect seems to make a distinct impact.

Daniel Goleman[1] (HBR Classic on Emotional Intelligence) grouped capabilities into three categories viz., purely technical capabilities (accounting, planning etc); cognitive capabilities (analytical reasoning, visioning, understanding the big picture and such others); and emotional intelligence (ability to lead change, work with others etc). When he ranked groups of highly effective leaders, he noticed that emotional intelligence was twice as important for jobs at all levels and played an increasingly crucial role at the higher levels of any organization, and nearly 90 percent difference in impact is attributable to this factor. He also identified five capabilities, which leaders should possess for better impact:

1. Self-awareness: confidence, self-assessment etc.
2. Self-regulation: trust, discipline, dealing with ambiguity etc.
3. Motivation: passion, energy, and optimism.
4. Empathy: attracting talent, developing others, sensitivity etc.
5. Social skill: persuasiveness, networking, building, and leading teams.

Importantly, emotional intelligence is a combination of inherent and acquired capability. Typically with varied experiences and maturity in dealing with many situations, people tend to build a strong emotional intelligence quotient.

Jon Gertner, author of *Idea Factory*, a book about Bell Labs[3], introduces John Pierce as an instigator. Pierce is an American engineer, who worked at Bell Labs in the areas of radio communication and microwave technology and he suggested the name 'Transistor' for the new device invented at Bell Labs in 1947. Gerner says, 'An instigator is different from a genius, but just as uncommon. An instigator is different, too, from the most skillful manager, some able to wrest excellence out of people who might otherwise fall short.' Pierce's real talent was 'in getting people interested in something that hadn't really occurred to them before'. That is another example of leadership of getting the best out of people within a given context.

In 1960s, Bell Labs engaged more than 1,200 PhDs and produced 13 Nobel Prize winners.

In this millennium, China's economic status is preeminent and has become central in the growth of the world economy. Undoubtedly, it is expected that the newly elected General Secretary of CPC Central Committee, Xi Jinping[4], will have an influential role to play. After the first plenary session of the 18th CPC Central Committee, Xi Jinping, delivered a refreshingly candid speech, bereft of political jargon, and embedded the people centered approach—'Our people have an ardent love for life. They wish to have better education, more stable jobs, more income, greater social security, better medical and health care, improved housing conditions, and a better environment. They want their children to have sound growth, have good jobs, and lead a more enjoyable life. To meet their desire for a happy life is our mission.' Though Xi's father, Xi Zhongxun, was a former CPC member, Xi never enjoyed any preferential treatment and during his teens, when his father was expelled during the 'cultural revolution' of 1966–1976, Xi moved to a small village in Shaanxi Province and toiled hard alongside farmers. He says, 'I worked 365 days a year, except when I was sick...on windy and rainy days, I cut hay in cave dwellings, and in the evening, I followed local villagers herding livestock. I did everything from herding sheep to carrying 100 kilogramme loads of wheat up mountain paths.' The hardship was to an extent alleviated by local villagers and perhaps that experience is the acquired emotional intelligence that has led him to think about serving the masses. During his tenure at Zhejiang, he visited 69 counties in nine months and often reminded officials to keep in mind that the government is the 'people's government'. The job carved out for him is not easy, but with people development in mind, he could perhaps surmount many obstacles.

It is important for leaders to have a people centric agenda on their mind because development of human capital is what really translates to economic activity. The context in this case is, China needs massive transformation and Xi is exerting his influence from the point of view of people orientation, perhaps a potent combination for delivering impact. Mobilization of the masses of a country as big as a continent, to accomplish goals—poverty eradication, education, means of self sustenance, economic activity leading to jobs, development of infrastructure, science and technology—needs a deep understanding of people issues and empathy to take action.

Richard Teerlink[6] took over as the CEO of Harley-Davidson in 1989, when the company had a 15 percent market share, was undergoing losses, and Japanese motorcycles were giving stiff competition to the US icon. In short, Harley was struggling. By the end of his tenure in 1997, Harley's US market share was 50 percent, and the annual sales were nearly $1.75 billion and then he went to serve on Harley-Davidson's Board until 2002. Teerlink achieved this transformation by focusing on people's ability to enhance quality, improved customer and dealer service, and worked on the designs to produce world class heavyweight motorcycles.

Michele Bodmer of Credit Suisse interviewed Teerlink in the winter of 2003. When asked, 'What were the most difficult steps in reinventing Harley-Davidson?' He replied, 'Getting leaders to believe that we needed to reinvent the company and recognizing that we, the leaders, were the problem. The biggest realization that Harley's leaders had to make was that they can no longer look at themselves as being the fountain of all wisdom, the world's best problem solvers, or the only ones who are responsible for its results. People as clients and employees are a company's only sustainable competitive advantage! When leaders understand this, the next step is to take responsibility for the operating environment that people walk into every day.' On culture, he said that five ingredients are very critical for transformation—awareness, individual responsibility, lifelong learning, involvement, and appreciation. Leaders should ask: How should we behave? What's important? Who do we serve? How do we measure success? Is the leader providing the resources to the people that work with him to be able to do their jobs? Is the leader ensuring that they have the opportunities to grow and develop? He says, 'One of the secrets is: ask the employee how he would like to be measured.' About brands he says, 'Brand is based on what an organization delivers to its stakeholders,' and in the case of Harley it was to fix the motorcycles to enhance its quality and reliability. Then it is communicated to the customer and a brand promise is created.

Many CEOs have focused on leadership and product transformation to gain market share and become profitable. What matters is realizing what it takes to get there. Often the stifling part of any major transformation is changing the mindsets of people from 'this is it', 'can't be done' to 'how do we get there'. The challenge faced by many leaders is an understanding of their self and how they can impact the company and the people. Steeped in the daily rigor of conducting business, they lose sight of the big opportunities and often relegate themselves to the mindset of status quo. That is why, many CEOs when they take up transformation work, weed out leadership at the senior levels and bring fresh talent from the market. Not because the existing leadership is low on competence, but because enormous efforts are needed to change mindsets of people and CEOs often don't have that much time at hand, especially when the boat has many holes in the bottom.

Entrepreneur magazine[5] in its Febuary 2013 article

writes that the adopted mantra of LinkedIn CEO Jeff Weiner is 'next play', a phrase borrowed from Duke basketball coach Mike Krzyzewski, who calls out after every sequence based on the move being offensive or defensive. Weiner explains it as, 'Take a minute to celebrate success or reflect on failure, but then move on.' Weiner acknowledges accomplishments but ends most of his meetings with the question, 'What he could have done better?' David Hahn, LinkedIn's VP of product management, says that Weiner works long hours, just like any other employee and that makes him a credible leader. As per an anonymous survey conducted by Glassdoor in 2012, LinkedIn was identified as one of the best places to work, with 92 percent employee approval rating. Hahn says, 'A big part of leadership and a big part of being a disciplined manager is being able to ask really great questions.' Weiner realizes that people do make mistakes and encourages it, 'The person who made the mistake or who can do better the next time leaves the meeting feeling good.'

LinkedIn is in the business of connecting people to network, learn, grow, and hopefully to seek opportunities for a better future. LinkedIn has fantastic innovation that has built incrementally with its unique product design features. Leadership is about consistently displaying results and growing the company to the next level. Often the CEO just shows the direction and the employees are motivated enough, because of the excitement surrounding the creation of a wonderful product, that they go for the best forms of execution.

Richard Clark[8] took over as CEO of Merck & Co. in 2005 when the arthritis drug Vioxx was pulled out off the market after reported side-effects of heart attack related deaths. During his tenure, he closed five manufacturing plants, cut upwards of 7,500 jobs, focused on new drug creation, and settled law suits worth $4.85 billion and Merck's stock price doubled from $35 to almost $70 per share. In the winter of 2008, Stephen Mcguire reported in Medical Marketing in Media, quoting Clarke's interview in *Wall Street Journal*, where he told employees, 'I am frustrated and you must be frustrated by what happened in the short-term, but be determined to deliver on our 2010 objectives.' In 2005, when Clarke stepped in, he defined a five year plan and went after it diligently and ensured that he didn't lose focus. While he made his view known to the external world, he was candid, and said, 'Our credibility in 2006 and 2007 was not misplaced; we'll have it again in 2008 and 2009.' He told the *Journal*, he was working on a new plan for 2011–2015, and added, 'Merck is in the midst of 150 products launches in different countries... but I have a full agenda... My responsibility is to take a long-term view, and not just a short-term one. The stock decline is a bump in the road, a setback, but our plan to win is long-term.'

In a 90 day season where Wall Street is breathing

down the necks of CEOs and boards, it needs confidence to take on some of the real issues head on and commit to a long term strategic view. The job of a CEO is very tough, especially during a transformation where the company is under the scanner of the public. To change perceptions of people, employees, and stakeholders needs sustained efforts. Quick restructuring, while it gives some initial results may not result in a sustained performance improvement. Depending upon the problems at hand, leaders have to prioritize the imminent ones and set them to rest, while in parallel work on recreating new ground. At times, the essence of leadership lies in what not to accomplish in the short-term and what to focus on in the long-term. There is no simple rule that determines this and the job of the leader is to figure this out.

Often, people respect CFOs and finance people for their extreme focus on number orientation and discredit them for their understanding of sensitivity and people. To that extent, the joke goes—when a financial analyst was sent for a classical philharmonic orchestra performance, he came back saying, 'Way too many people playing the same tune on similar violin, why don't they prune?' But then there are exceptions. Lawrence Keller[2] joined as the CFO of Continental Airlines in 1995, when Gordon Bethune was the CEO of the beleaguered Airlines which was losing nearly $55 million a month. He quickly worked out a refinance plan, pioneering an air-fleet-backed-bond, which helped Continental to raise money cheaply. He calculated that the airline would save $6 million a month, if it increased its customer satisfaction ranking to fifth place. He created a plan to give employees $3 million a month to motivate them to improve the 'on time' ranking. Continental airlines shot from the last place to the first place in just 60 days! Together with Bethune, in his first couple of years at Continental, they put the company back on the financial track by turning it around from a loss of $600 million to clocking net profit of $224 million and by squeezing out $1.1 billion in costs. Within a few years, in 2004, he took over as the CEO, upon Bethune's retirement. During his tenure as the CEO, more than ability to understand numbers, he was respected for his ability to communicate with Continental's 45,000 employees and bring them on board to ensure better customer satisfaction levels.

Keller's leadership style was practical—cutting costs, motivating employees, refinancing and going after the metrics, because the need of the hour was to save the planes from getting grounded forever. Incidentally, Continental was one of the few airlines that saved itself from going bankrupt.

Again leadership's other dimension is to see, given a certain moment in the history of a company, what works the best. At times, it is change in leadership, at times, it has to do with operational strategies and sometimes it is crystal gazing into the future. Often quick-fix operational strategies are applied such as cost-cutting, refinancing, reducing head count, and such others, when the company is going through losses and when cash flow is being stretched. So, the market and the current state of affairs might dictate the CEOs priorities even though leaders might want to work on long-term value propositions. Leaders, who can balance the short and long-term, lead the company to a brighter future.

Mary Kay Ash[9,10], Founder of May Kay Cosmetics said, 'Pretend that every single person you meet has a sign around his or her neck that says "Make Me Feel Important". Not only will you succeed in business, you will succeed in life.' The practice of rewarding her top consultants (employees) with Pink Cadillacs started in 1969, and as of today, about 9,000 women drive these cadillacs, valued at almost $140 million, that constitutes the largest commercial fleet of GM's passenger cars in the world. Hers was the only company to be featured thrice on Fortune's list of 100 Best Companies to Work For in America and she is the only woman business leader profiled in *Forbes*' Greatest Business Stories of All Time.

Mary Kay stumbled upon her sales abilities when in

1930s, a door-to-door saleswoman who sold encyclopedias struck a deal with Mary that she could have one free if she helped sell ten of them. Mary sold them in a day and half, which usually took 90 days for people to sell. Soon, she started selling the books and managed to support her family. Her friends said that she was selling what they didn't need. So she joined Stanley Home Products where she sold house wares, but soon hit the glass ceiling seeing much less talented men get promoted, she resigned in frustration. Then she went and joined the direct sales firm World Gift Co., and within a decade, she expanded the company to 43 states and became a part of its board. But much to her chagrin, her male counterparts dismissed her suggestions with the comment, 'Oh, Mary Kay, you are thinking just like a woman,' and this remark stayed with her, as she finally quit, because a man she trained was promoted to be her supervisor with twice the salary. After quitting she decided to retire and write about her experiences to help other women, so that they could succeed in a male-dominated corporate world. She composed two lists viz., her negative experiences and second an ideal business environment where women could thrive. As she wrote, she realized that instead of theorizing, why not start something? So she started off by using $5000 of her savings and started a skin care product, which was based on a tanner's formula and opened a small store in Dallas. She worked the direct sales model where her employees called consultants would show women how to use the cosmetic product to improve appearance and the results would enhance sales. It worked brilliantly. In 90 days the company earned $34,000 and by the end of the first year sales were nearly $2,00,000. Within a year she touched $8,00,000 with 3,000 consultants. In 1968, the company went public and by 1983, sales rose to $324 million and shareholders started questioning her about the pink cars being given to the consultants, which were her prime motivational tool and a symbol of success for many women. Instead of cutting back on the Cadillac incentive programme, in 1985, she took the company private. In 1993, the company hit the $1 billion mark and as on 2008, the company has more than 1.7 million consultants worldwide and revenues in excess of $2.2 billion. Her belief in 'God first, family second, and career third', combined with her efforts resulted in a multi-level direct sales driven cosmetic firm where millions of women benefited.

Leadership is belief in what you stand for and taking it to fruition. Interestingly, Mary Kay started her sales career when she first met the door-to-door sales woman, but didn't think of starting her firm until her mid-forties, when she turned a writing experience into a world class company. The story of Mary Kay is one of ingenuity, determination, hard work, courage, and a never give up attitude. She took each situation that she was confronted with, to the next level of success, and that is the personality trait of a fighter, a leader who has the energy and tenacity to make things happen.

Leadership comes in all forms, in different shapes and dimensions, with evolving stages of every company. Appropriately leaders, bring in their emotional, cognitive and technical competencies to give shape to their thoughts and the eventual outcome. The key learning is that the same shoe doesn't fit all. Sometimes it may not even need a shoe and at times even a store full of shoes may not suffice.

HUMILITY

'True humility is not thinking less of yourself; it is thinking of yourself less.'

—C.S. Lewis

USUALLY THEY SAY THAT the last chapter should come with a bang, a twist in the tale, something that the reader or the viewer takes home. So I was wondering what topic to delve into. Many important ones such as 'managing relationships', 'living with conflicts', 'understanding paradoxes', and such others vied with each other to take their place as the last set of nuggets to be sown. But somehow, I wasn't convinced and thought that I should settle for a completely different topic and upon conferring with a few friends from the industry, I hit upon 'humility' as the topic to wrap up this book.

We all know about the importance of humility, but

do you why I included it as the last chapter? Because it is absolutely rare and one hardly sees it!

My job comprises meeting people, providing consulting services, working along with them, making them and their companies succeed, and it is real fun because as a third party, I get to see so many facets of people—desires, aspirations, desperations, ambiguities, anxieties, need for power, recognition, use and control of resources, and what not. But honestly, I get to see very little humility. Not that people are bad or brazen or arrogant at what they do and accomplish, but because many don't seem to realize or stop in their tracks and think. This is primarily because they don't have time to reflect and ponder. They perhaps want to accomplish too many things in too short a time—the pressures of corporate working is so.

Often, people relate success to what they have done and failure to what others have done to them. I hear people talk about 'I did this…I did that…I was there…I pioneered it…I made it happen…I was instrumental…I achieved the result…I made the transformation happen'. But in reality, none of these accomplishments can ever happen without teamwork and without people around making it happen for others. Before we get wrong notions about humility, let me quickly quote from a HBR blog network article, 'Six Principles for Developing Humility as a Leader' by John Dame and Jeffery Gedmin, September 9, 2013. 'Humility is not hospitality, courtesy, or a kind and friendly demeanor. Humility has nothing to do with being meek, weak, or indecisive. Perhaps more surprisingly, it does not entail shunning publicity. Organizations need people who get marketing, including self-marketing, to flourish and prosper.'

Humility is much deeper, it is about the way a leader behaves or a manager acts to get the best out of his people for the better of their organization and communities, without really conveying self-aggrandizement. To reiterate, according to the Taoist philosopher, Lao Tzu, 'A leader is best when people barely know he exists, when his work is done, his aim fulfilled, they will say, we did it ourselves.' In a way principles of Taoism have integrated leadership with a deep sense of humility. When I read the philosophy, it occurred to me that 'attainment' was given precedence over 'achievement', because the former was about sublime communion and the latter stoked individuality.

At times it is difficult to integrate an idealistic approach with business objectives such as profitability. But then recently when I went to visit the Merck office in Mumbai, I came across a quote by George Wilheim Merck, president of the American pharmaceutical manufacturing company. He said in his address to the medical college of Virginia, Richmond on December 1, 1950, 'We try never to forget that medicine is for the people. It is not for the profits. The profits follow, and if we have remembered that, they have never failed to appear. The better we have remembered it, the larger they have been.' Inspiring business leaders and companies have always focused on the larger cause of serving people, which helped them create sustainable growth companies because the philosophies of such companies has been ingrained in the humility of service.

In spite of millions of books and articles being written on this topic, people still somehow cannot seem to forsake the word 'I' and replace it with the word 'we'. That is the truth and the reality of life that we all tend to miss. In the process, we trample, do not recognize those small contributions, a smile there, a nice word here, and importantly, we are too busy caught up with finishing our tasks, getting things done, and getting back to the same tomorrow—*the never ending rat-race*. Very few have taken time to thank, show gratitude and to make institutions of their deeds. Here is an inspiring example of humility that I came across on one of sulekha.com's[1] blogs on the topic of inspiration and humility.

'Zavere Poonawala is a well-known Parsi industrialist from Pune. Ganga Datt was his driver for thirty years and one fine day passed away. At the time of his demise, Mr Poonawala was in Mumbai attending some official work. As soon as he heard the news of his driver's death, he cancelled all his meetings, requested the driver's family to wait for him for the cremation, and rushed to Pune by a helicopter. On reaching Pune, he asked the limo to be decorated with flowers as he wished Ganga Datt should be taken in the same car, which he drove for the last thirty years. When Ganga Datt's family agreed to his wishes, he himself drove Ganga Datt from his home up to the ghat (funeral place on the banks of a river) on his last journey. When asked about his gesture, Mr Poonawala replied that Ganga Datt had served him day and night, and the least he could do is to be eternally grateful to him. He further added that Ganga Datt rose up from poverty and educated both his children very well. His daughter is a chartered accountant and that is so commendable. He added, "Everybody earns money and there is nothing unusual in that, but we should always be grateful to those people who contribute to our success. This is the belief, we have been brought up with, which made me do, what I did".'

Here is an interesting quote from Abraham Lincoln: 'I have been driven many times upon my knees by the overwhelming conviction that I had nowhere else to go. My own wisdom and that of all about me seemed insufficient for that day.' Humility is about asking for help. Many of us keep at it and do not shout or ask for help. I remember one of the early discussions we had during our Alcatel–Lucent merger days about people adapting to newer ways of doing things, understanding and adapting to each other's products and services. Almost everybody was trying to solve a problem, which probably had already been attempted. Not many raised their hands and asked questions, it could be the fear of asking or it could be that culturally people were not comfortable asking questions. Most fear that the question could be silly, despite strong reinforcement since kindergarten that no question is stupid.

Humility is also about helping others in need. Here is another interesting story. In the 18th century, in Baltimore, on a stormy night, a tree uprooted and fell on a road. A team of soldiers was assigned to clear the log. They tried moving the log, but it didn't budge. Then they started cutting the branches and clearing the way, but still it did not work. Meanwhile the senior officer on his horseback was giving stern orders, commanding the soldiers on how they should be clearing the way. A passerby saw what was happening and asked the senior officer, why he couldn't lend a hand. To which, the superior officer replied that he was the officer in command and it was below his dignity to work along with the soldiers. The traveller nodded, removed his coat, rolled his sleeves, and got to work with the soldiers. They toiled for hours and finally were able to move the trunk and clear the way. After the work was done, the traveller who was about to leave said, 'When you have difficult work, call on me, I will come to help you'. The commanding officer asked, 'Who are you?' Before galloping off, the stranger said, 'I am George Washington.' The stranger was none other than the first president of America and the commander-in-chief of the US military.

Displaying humility is never below one's dignity, but sadly many are mistaken. Here is an excerpt from a letter that Mahatma Gandhi wrote on February 14, 1911 at Tolstoy farm, to Maganlal Gandhi, who was an associate of Gandhi between 1903–1928. 'I am mostly busy making sandals these days. I have already made 15 pairs. When you need one, please send me the measurements. And when you do so, mark the places where the strap is to be fixed—that is on the outer side of the big toe and the little one.' And at Sabarmati Ashram, Gandhiji had taken it upon himself to clean the public toilets.

People with humility ingrained in them often lead the same lifestyles they were used to before they made their billions. They are not insecure, are comfortable with, their surroundings, the people they work and live with and often help in community initiatives and social programmes. Though they might be billionaires and can dish out a lot more dollars or can afford much more, often they are not ostentatious and stick to their business principles and the fundamentals they carved out for themselves during their early stages of life. Here are a few examples.[2]

- Amancio Ortega is the founder of Zara and is a billionaire. He and his wife still live in a discreet apartment building in La Coruna, Spain. He wears the same uniform every day, eats lunch with employees, and visits the same coffee shop every day.

- Azim Premji, India's IT czar and a self-made billionaire still travels coach class and is very prudent about costs.
- Warren Buffet still lives in the same house he bought some fifty years ago for $31,500. He feels that expensive gadgets and toys are a pain in the neck.
- David Green is the billionaire founder of Hobby Lobby and has become the largest individual donor for evangelical causes in the US.
- Chuck Feeney's (cofounder of Duty Free Shoppers) net worth is currently $2 million because he has donated more than $4 billion to disadvantaged children and public health initiatives. And he never wanted people to know that he had donated pretty much all his money.

It does not mean that people with charitable minds or people who live by frugal means are humble. It may be or may not be. However, it is often reported that people who have cultivated humility are sensitive to other's needs, are compassionate, and often live by simple means, despite their ability to afford much more.

The antithesis of humility is robust individualism, tending towards arrogance and in extreme instances leading to narcissism. I have come across individuals who cannot think of anything beyond themselves and the only way to get things done and keep them engaged is to keep stroking their ego and get them hooked to larger-than-life goals, which will contain their energy and orientation. When the fear of failure sets in, people always tend to step back a bit and think it through. At times, I also introduce them to people who have accomplished much more in their lives and are very humble—in the hope that they will learn from others. The flip side of this scale is 'servility'. I also come across people who are utterly servile and are not able to manage the power equations well. At times, people really stoop to levels where others start taking advantage of them. Again, that is not humility. Humility is a state of an egoless mind, being cognizant of the boundaries in managing relationships, the perceptions around, and importantly focusing on the outcomes. But then there is no set rule in all these and one has to figure it out based on the context.

To inculcate a sense of context and self-awareness, coaching is a good option that many senior executives pursue. Fast Company[3] reports that 43 percent CEOs and 71 percent senior executives say that they have worked with a coach. Of this, 92 percent leaders are willing to use the services of a coach once again. I coach many CEOs and senior management executives and find that most of them are willing to listen, though many find it difficult to change behaviours in a short period, especially those habits that have been acquired over a long period of time. Interestingly, I have been telling one of the senior people I coach, to speak less and to be less of a micromanager in trying to get to the results. Because whenever he gets into a roll, there is no gap between what he thinks and what he speaks, and the endless questions he poses. This lands him into many unwanted people issues. Now, how does one curb such behaviour quickly? Obviously it is going to take time before he can change, but now he is aware and being self-aware is half the battle won.

Humility is something that a person carries, cultivates as part of his leadership persona, and enshrines it in his personal and professional ecosystem. And this habit has the tendency to percolate and spread. People with humility are far more respected, are listened to, make better managers and leaders, and importantly can make transformative changes much easier than most others who are not. This is because a humble person is everybody's apple-pie. One does not have to make special efforts to cultivate relationships; for people with humility in their hearts, relationships happen faster and last longer, because there is no ego fight and marking of territories. At the end of the day, it has to be remembered that 'people care for those who care for them'.

Let me end with an example. A bunch of fourth graders were given a game to play. A balloon was tied to one of the legs of each child and they were expected to stomp out each other's balloons until only one remained, and that child would be declared the winner. As soon as the game was announced, children pounded, pushed, pounced on each other, until one child emerged the winner, and she turned to be the most hated child, by the rest of the children for the entire term.

A similar exercise was given to a bunch of special children. And as soon as the whistle was blown, each of them offered their balloon to be stomped by holding up their respective balloons and by the end of the game all balloons were stomped and the children clapped when the last balloon was popped. Nobody emerged winner and all emerged winners. Either they didn't understand the game or played it the way they saw it.

The important question is: What do you want to do? Which game do you want to play? And is it worth it?

Notes and References

Introduction

1. Malcolm Gladwell Books, *Outliers*, Allen Lane, Penguin Group, 2008, US.

Failures to Success

1. Melissa A. Venable, PhD, '50 Famously Successful People Who Failed at First'. www.onlinecollege.org
2. Nelson Mandela. http://en.wikipedia.org/wiki/Nelson_Mandela
3. Wikipedia, The *Time* Magazine, '100 Most Important People of the Century'. About Oprah Gail Winfrey: http://en.wikipedia.org/wiki/Time_100:_The_Most_Important_People_of_the_Century

4. Sydney Poiter. http://en.wikipedia.org/wiki/Sidney_Poitier
5. Jack Andraka, 'Many Rejections to Success'. http://en.wikipedia.org/wiki/Jack_Andraka

Play to Strengths

1. Rick Karlgaard, Peter Drucker, 'Leadership', November 19, 2004. http://www.forbes.com/2004/11/19/cz_rk_1119drucker.html
2. Steve Denning on Peter Drucker, 'The Founder of the Twenty First Century Management', Peter Drucker, *Forbes* Online, March 01, 2013. http://www.forbes.com/sites/stevedenning/2013/03/01/the-founder-of-21st-century-management-peter-drucker/
3. Peter Drucker (Classic), 'Managing Oneself', *Harvard Business Review*, Aug-Dec, 2012.
4. Rosa Parks, 'Adult Life of Rosa Parks', 'The Day on the Bus', April 7, 2006. http://historyday13.tripod.com/id5.html
5. Article, 'The 100 Best CEOs in the World, '*Harvard Business Review*, Jan-Feb 2013.
6. Elizabeth Haas Edersheim, 'The Definitive Drucker', Mcgraw Hill, 2007, US.

Human Experience

1. 'The Power of Design' (about IDEO), *Bloomberg Business Week*. http://www.businessweek.com/stories/2004-05-16/the-power-of-design
2. Tom Kelley and David Kelley, 'Reclaim Your Creative Confidence', '*Harvard Business Review*', Dec 2012. http://hbr.org/2012/12/reclaim-your-creative-confidence
3. Walter Isaacson, 'The Real Leadership Lessons of Steve Jobs', *Harvard Business Review*, April 2012.
4. Danielle Sacks, Denny's to Charmin, 'Brands Try to Crack the Social Conversation' (and about Redbull), *Fast Company* online, Jan 15, 2013. http://www.fastcompany.com/3004364/dennys-charmin-brands-try-crack-social-conversation
5. 'Listen Up and Speak', *Fast Company*, Feb 2013.
6. June 2012 issue, *Fast Company*, on Rebecca Van Dyck.
7. *Fast Company*, Feb 2013, on Michael Migliozzi

Common Sense

1. 'The Billionaire's Apprentice', 'The Rise of the Indian American Elite and the Fall of the Galleon Hedge Fund', Anita Raghavan, 2013, Hachette Book Group Inc.
2. Dakin Sloss, 'Common Sense for California:

Stanford Group Works to Fix Government with Data', *Huffington Post*, Aug 24, 2011. http://www.huffingtonpost.com/dakinsloss/post_2341_b_935612.html

3. Dr Edwin M Glasscock, Phd, 'Common Sense The # 1 Critical Success Factor, It's Not Rocket Science'. *iUniverse*, 2005, US.
4. Nassim Nicholas Talib, 'Anti Fragile', Allen Lane, Penguin Group 2012, US.
5. Jonathan Mantle, 'Companies that Changed the World: From East India Company to Google Inc', Quercus Publishing Plc, London 2008.
6. Fred Greenstein, 'How Do Historians Evaluate the Administration of Dwight Eisenhower?' July 8, 2002, *History* News Network. http://hnn.us/articles/441.html

Intuition

1. Rick Karlgaard, Peter Drucker, 'Leadership', November 19, 2004. http://www.forbes.com/2004/11/19/cz_rk_1119drucker.html
2. Steve Denning on Peter Drucker, 'The Founder of the Twenty First Century Management', Peter Drucker, *Forbes* Online, March 01, 2013. http://www.forbes.com/sites/stevedenning/2013/03/01/the-founder-of-21st-century-management-peter-drucker/
3. Peter Drucker (Classic), 'Managing Oneself, *Harvard*

Business Review, Aug-Dec, 2012.

4. Viswanathan Anand's lecture at 'Lecture on Chessdom', June 26, 2012. http://www.chessdom.com/world-champion-viswanathan-anand-gives-lecture-on-return-on-analytics/
5. Daniel Kahneman, Nobel Laureate in Economics, 'Thinking Fast and Thinking Slow', Allen Lane, Penguin Group, 2011, US.
6. '50 Ideas You Really Need to Know: Psychology', Prof. Adrian Furnham, Quercus Publishing Plc, London 2007, 2012.
7. About Amar Gopal Bose, Wikipedia article, http://en.wikipedia.org/wiki/Bose_Corporation
8. Micheal A. Roberto, Richard M. J. Bohmer, Amy C. Edmondson, 'Facing Ambiguous Threats', *HBR*, Nov 2006. http://hbr.org/2006/11/facing-ambiguous-threats/ar/1

Leap of Faith

1. Wiki article about Redbull. http://en.wikipedia.org/wiki/Red_Bull
2. Wiki article about the story of Allen Lane. http://en.wikipedia.org/wiki/Allen_Lane
3. Kristin Laird, Marketer of the Year 2012, 'McDonald's Canada, Marketing, Advertising and PR in Canada'.

Jan 23, 2013. http://www.marketingmag.ca/news/marketer-news/marketer-of-the-year-2012-mcdonalds-canada-70067

4. *Fast Company*, June 2012, story on Ma Jun

Unlearning

1. Erica Dhawan, 'Business Schools Need to Focus on Unlearning', *Forbes*, online, June 13, 2012. http://www.brainfriendlytrainer.com/reflect/10-fantastic-quotes-about-unlearning
2. 'Unlearning 101: Unlearning is Uncomfortable', Jack Uldrich, July 22, 2010. http://www.unlearning101.com/fuhgetaboutit_the_art_of_/2010/07/unlearning-is-uncomfortable.html

Listening

3. Article, 'The 100 Best CEOs in the World, '*Harvard Business Review*, Jan-Feb 2013.
4. John Ryan, 'Center for Creative Leadership: Every CEO Must be a Chief Listening Officer, *Forbes* Online, Dec 30, 2009. http://www.forbes.com/2009/12/30/chief-listening-officer-leadership-managing-ccl.html
5. '101 Zen Stories', 'Buddha's Zen: The Story'. http://www.101zenstories.com/index.php?story=101

Innovation

1. Austin Carr, 'World's Most Innovative Companies', *Fast Company* online, Jan 2013. http://www.fastcompany.com/section/most-innovative-companies-2013
2. '100 Most Creative People in Business', *Fast Company*, June 2012.
3. Article on Pinterest, Wikipedia. http://en.wikipedia.org/wiki/Pinterest
4. Ari Levy, Pinterest valued at $2.5 billion following investment from Valiant, *Bloomberg Business Week*, Feb 21, 2013. http://www.bloomberg.com/news/2013-02-21/pinterest-gets-200-million-in-funding-at-2-5-billion-valuation.html
5. Wiki Source of *Encyclopedia Britannia* on the story of Thomas Cook. http://en.wikisource.org/wiki/1911_Encyclopper centC3per centA6dia_Britannica/Cook,_Thomas
6. Amy Ryles, 'Using Criticism to Fuel Innovation', *eatbigfish.com*, Jan 11, 2013 on the story of Nicholas Negroponte. http://eatbigfish.com/theblog/innovation-blog/using-criticism-to-fuel-innovation
7. About Ekso Bionics, article on Wikipedia. http://en.wikipedia.org/wiki/Ekso_Bionics
8. Will Omerus, About Ekso Bionics, *Concord Monitor*, March 22, 2013. http://www.concordmonitor.com/news/nation/world/5256243-95/ekso-exoskeletons-

woo-angold

9. Robyn Waters, 'The Hummer and the Mini: Navigating the Contradictions of the New Trend Landscape', Portfolio, Penguin, 2006, US.

Happiness

1. Dr David Myers Lecture on TVU. http://tv.up.pt/videos/H6Gj46Lo
2. Eric L Zielinski Research on 'Happiness Offers Clues to the Abundant Life', *Natural News*, March 23, 2013. http://www.naturalnews.com/039605_happiness_abundance_mindset.html referenced from other sources - http://camsolivia.hubpages.com http://www.boston.com, http://www.psychologytoday.com, http://internal.psychology.illinois.edu,http://internal.psychology.illinois.edu, http://www.youtube.com/watch?v=7qSdZPAybf0, http://www.youtube.com/watch?v=WaHO1OHNc2s, http://latimesblogs.latimes.com
3. Chapter Happiness – Article about Happiness Economics on Wikipedia reference - http://en.wikipedia.org/wiki/Happiness_economics
4. Article about 'Happiness Economics' on Wikipedia. http://en.wikipedia.org/wiki/Satisfaction_with_Life_Index
5. Carolanne Wright, 'Seeking the Key to Happiness?'

Research suggests taming the wandering mind, April 12, 2013. http://www.naturalnews.com/039886_happiness_meditation_thoughts.html

6. Matt Killingsworth, 'Ted Talk: Want to be happier, Stay in the Moment', Nov 2011. http://www.ted.com/talks/matt_killingsworth_want_to_be_happier_stay_in_the_moment.html
7. Matt Killingsworth, 'Want to be Happier, Stay in the Moment', (paper consisting of methodology, data, question details). http://www.wjh.harvard.edu/~dtg/KILLINGSWORTHper cent20&per cent20GILBERTper cent20(2010).pdf
8. Marla Popova, 'The Daily Routines of Famous Writers'. http://www.brainpickings.org/index.php/2012/11/20/daily-routines-writers/
9. Albert Costill, AMOG, Alpha Male of the Group, April 12, 2013. http://amog.com/lifestyle/156702-study-shows-tweeters-happier-travel/
10. Prof. David D Myers, 'Close Relationships and Quality of Life, Well Being : The foundation of Hedonic Psychology', New York, Russell Sage Foundation. http://www.davidmyers.org/davidmyers/assets/Close.Relationships.pdf
11. Elizabeth Scott, MS, Happiness Research, Here are some happiness research results you should know about. Jan 17, 2013, *About.com* Health, Stress

Management. http://stress.about.com/od/research/a/Happiness-Research.htm

12. John M Grohol, PSYD, '5 Reliable Findings from Happiness Research', *Psych Central*. http://psychcentral.com/blog/archives/2010/04/10/5-reliable-findings-from-happiness-research/
13. 'Mom was Wrong: Money Does Buy Happiness'. There is research to prove it. Abram Brown, *Forbes* Online, Jan 11, 2013. http://www.forbes.com/sites/abrambrown/2013/01/11/mom-was-wrong-money-does-indeed-buy-happiness-theres-research-to-prove-it/
14. George Chachrouri, 'Summary of Dr Kahneman', 'The Sad Tale of Aspiration', *docstoc.com*. http://www.docstoc.com/docs/91234347/Summary-of-Dr-Daniel-Kahneman_-The-Sad-Tale-of-the-Aspiration-
15. Jill Blessing, 'What is Hedonic Treadmill?' *Livestrong.com*, Oct 25, 2010. http://www.livestrong.com/article/289049-what-is-the-hedonic-treadmill/
16. Laura Rowley, 'The Hedonic Treadmill: The More We Have, The More We Want', *Money and Happiness*. http://www.moneyandhappiness.com/blog/?p=408
17. Jamie Hale, 'What Makes Us Happy?' *Psych Central*. http://psychcentral.com/lib/2011/what-makes-us-happy/
18. About Zappos Company culture that delivers happiness. http://enviableworkplace.com/case-study-zappos-company-culture-delivers-happiness/#axzz2RPOYevxA

Advocacy

1. 'The 100 Most Influential People in the World', *Time* Magazine, April-May 2013.
2. Jody Williams, 1997 Nobel Laureate, *www.peacejam.com*, 'Change Starts Here'. http://www.peacejam.org/laureates/Jody-Williams-11.aspx
3. About Jody Williams. http://www.icbl.org/intro.php
4. About Jody Williams, Wikipedia article reference. http://en.wikipedia.org/wiki/Jody_Williams
5. 'Why CEOs Oppose HIV Travel Ban: They Are Bad for Business'. http://www.huffingtonpost.com/chip-bergh/hiv-travel-ban_b_2200381.html
6. 'CEOs Advocate for the End of Travel Restrictions for People Living with HIV'. http://www.gbchealth.org/news-article/613-CEO_pledge_to_end_travel_restrictions_for_people_living_with_hiv/#CEOs
7. *www.allstate.com*, company website on how they are reducing teen accidents with peer to peer advocacy.
8. 'Completed Projects on Traffic Safety'. https://www.aaafoundation.org/research/completed-projects
9. Liu Xiaboa. http://en.wikipedia.org/wiki/Liu_Xiaobo

Philanthropy

1. Philanthropy. http://en.wikipedia.org/wiki/Harvard_University

2. About creation of Stanford University. http://www.stanford.edu/about/history
3. About creation of Stanford University. http://en.wikipedia.org/wiki/MIT_Sloan_School_of_Management
4. Maria Di Mento, *Philanthropy 50*, 'The Chronicle of Philanthropy', Feb 10, 2013. http://philanthropy.com/article/No-2-Mark-Zuckerberg-and/137137/
5. *Philanthropy 50*, 'A Strong Showing for Donors Under 40', 'The Chronicle of Philanthropy', Feb 10, 2013. http://philanthropy.com/section/Facts-Figures/235/
6. 'The 50 Most Generous Philanthropists'. http://www.businessweek.com/interactive_reports/philanthropy_individual.html
7. *Forbes* 400: 'Billionaires Who have Signed the Giving Pledge'. http://www.forbes.com/pictures/ekeg45mff/warren-buffett/
8. 'The 50 Most Generous Philanthropists', *Bloomberg Business Week*, http://images.businessweek.com/ss/07/11/1115_philanthropy/index_01.htm
9. Warren Buffet in Wikipedia reference. http://en.wikipedia.org/wiki/Warren_Buffett
10. *www.givingpledge.org*, for letters and other details of Warren Buffet, Manoj Bhargava, David Rockefeller, Azim Premji and related references to Philanthropy.
11. http://www.rockefellerfoundation.org/

Diversity

1. References of CISCO Chambers views and the CISCO Inclusive advocacy. http://www.cisco.com/web/about/ac49/ac55/docs/IAP_AAG.pdf, http://www.cisco.com/web/about/ac49/ac55/docs/IAP_Profile.pdf
2. 'Diversity at Work Case Studies'. http://www.diversityatwork.net/EN/en_case_company.htm
3. 'Working Mother, 100 Best Companies to Work in 2012'.
4. http://www.workingmother.com/best-companies/cisco-9
5. '85broads, A Global Women's Network'. http://www.85broads.com/
6. Kraftfoods in Diversity Inc's top 50. http://www.diversityinc.com/kraft-foods
7. For interviews with people at Wells Fargo, http://www.diversityinc.com/
8. http://www.guardian.co.uk/world/2013/may/22/german-it-firm-sap-seeks-autistic-workers

Situational Leadership

1. Daniel Goleman (Classic), 'What Makes A Leader?' *Harvard Business Review*, Aug-Dec 2012.
2. '1000 CEOs: *Proven Strategies for Success from the World's Smartest Executives*', Editor in Chief, Andre

Davidson, Dorling Kindersley, Great Britain, 2009.
3. Innovation at Bell Labs. http://www.leadershipnow.com/leadingblog/2012/06/innovation_at_bell_labs.html
4. Su Yuan, 'The Third Angle', *gbtimes*, Jan 4, 2013. http://gbtimes.com/focus/politics/chinese-media/xi-jinping-people-centric-leader
5. Stephanie Vozza, '10 Inspirational Leaders Who Turned Around Their Companies', *Entrepreneur.com*, Feb 22, 2013. http://www.entrepreneur.com/slideshow/225890
6. Interview with Richard Teerlink of Harley Davidson. https://infocus.creditsuisse.com/app/article/index.cfm?fuseaction=OpenArticle&aoid=27009&coid=162&lang=EN
7. '5 Influential Leaders Weigh In On What Makes A Good Leader', *Entrepreneur.com* , Feb 25, 2013. http://www.entrepreneur.com/article/225804
8. Stephen Mcguire, Merck CEO to WSJ, 'I am frustrated'. *Medical Marketing and Media*, March 25, 2008. http://www.mmm-online.com/merck-CEO-to-wsj iamfrustrated/article/108300/
9. Mary Kay Ash. 'A Beauty Queen Opens Up the World of Entrepreneurship to Tens and Thousands of Women', Oct 10, 2008. http://www.entrepreneur.com/article/197602

10. Article on Wikipedia on Mary Kay Ash. http://en.wikipedia.org/wiki/Mary_Kay

Humility

1. A blog on *Sulekha* about Zavere Poonawala and Ganga Datt. http://creative.sulekha.com/mr-zavere-poonawala-and-ganga-datt_602390_blog
2. http://addicted2success.com/news/15-super-rich-billionaires-who-stay-grounded-humble/
3. http://blogs.hbr.org/2013/09/six-principles-for-developing/

ACKNOWLEDGEMENTS

THIS BOOK WOULDN'T HAVE been possible, if people, especially clients, colleagues, professionals, executives, friends, and family hadn't shared their stories and wonderful life experiences. I am really thankful to you all for sharing a little space of yours with me. Thank you for those wondrous moments, playful banters, shared paths, uproarious brickbats, unequivocal disagreements, upbeat times, umpteen meetings, regaling dinners, momentous occasions, quiet lows, bright days, and above all for the silent prayers and sincere conversations. Thank you for being there. All of you make the journey worthwhile.

While researching for the book, to convey insights and many point of views, I voraciously read many books, business and generic magazines, newspaper articles, research and academic papers, referred to generic and company internet websites, Wikipedia, other encyclopedias, collected trivia and interesting stories, and wherever possible, I have used publicly available information and given the reference and due credit to the researchers, professors, editors, writers, speakers, bloggers, magazines, online sites, and teams of people who worked hard and created volumes of rich information, and if I missed a reference, it is purely inadvertent. Without these writings and references from these thought leaders who have paved way for all of us to learn, it would not have been possible for me to write this book, which primarily relied on secondary and tertiary information, analysis, and anecdotal evidence from these many sources. I express my sincere gratitude to each one of them.

A Note on the Author

TGC PRASAD IS THE bestselling author of *Unusual People Do Things Differently* (Penguin, Portfolio), *From the Eye of My Mind* (Random House, Ebury), and *Along the Way* (Rupa Publishers).

He is on the advisory board of several companies, and works as a managing partner of TGC Consulting (www.tgc-consulting.com), a human capital consulting firm offering three services viz., Executive: Search, Coaching, and Advisory to Global MNCs, Transnational Indian conglomerates, and PE/VC funded entrepreneurial ventures across geographies such as Americas, Europe, Asia Pacific, and Australia.

He is an avid blogger and you can read his blogs on: http://tgcblogs.wordpress.com